TREMORS
IN THE
UNIVERSE

A Personal Journey of Discovery
with Parkinson's Disease and Spirituality

ROBERT LYMAN BAITTIE

BALBOA.
PRESS
A DIVISION OF HAY HOUSE

Cover and interior image by Bob Baittie Design, Inc

Balboa Press books may be ordered through booksellers or by contacting:

Balboa Press
A Division of Hay House
1663 Liberty Drive
Bloomington, IN 47403
www.balboapress.com
1 (877) 407-4847

Because of the dynamic nature of the Internet, any web addresses or links contained in this book may have changed since publication and may no longer be valid. The views expressed in this work are solely those of the author and do not necessarily reflect the views of the publisher, and the publisher hereby disclaims any responsibility for them.

The author of this book does not dispense medical advice or prescribe the use of any technique as a form of treatment for physical, emotional, or medical problems without the advice of a physician, either directly or indirectly. The intent of the author is only to offer information of a general nature to help you in your quest for emotional and spiritual well-being. In the event you use any of the information in this book for yourself, which is your constitutional right, the author and the publisher assume no responsibility for your actions.

Any people depicted in stock imagery provided by Thinkstock are models, and such images are being used for illustrative purposes only.
Certain stock imagery © Thinkstock.

Printed in the United States of America.

ISBN: 978-1-4525-2014-8 (sc)
ISBN: 978-1-4525-2016-2 (hc)
ISBN: 978-1-4525-2015-5 (e)

Library of Congress Control Number: 2014914998

Balboa Press rev. date: 9/17/2014

DEDICATION

FOR MY FAMILY ~ THE SUM OF ALL LOVE

Debbie, Amanda, Erica & Adam
Mom & Dad
Tom, Lisa, Lindsay & Courtney
Stu & Marcy
Dan, Joyce, Melissa, Jessica & Jamie
Mike, Judy, Rebecca & Jack

And for my grandfather Lyman:
Thank you for giving me your smile.

Well I am certainly wiser than this man. It is only too likely that neither of us has any knowledge to boast of; but he thinks that he knows something which he does not know, whereas I am quite conscious of my ignorance. At any rate it seems that I am wiser than he is to this small extent that I do not think that I know what I do not know.

~Socrates

PREFACE

Tremors in the Universe is a deeply personal chronicle of my quest to discover spiritual balance in my life as Parkinson's disease threatens to destroy my balance physically.

Initiated as a blog sixteen months after receiving my diagnosis, my intention in journaling my thoughts and experiences was threefold: to provide myself the opportunity for thoughtful introspection where a greater understanding of my relationship with Parkinson's and my spirituality might be achieved; to provide my three children with a more complete picture of their fathers beliefs and perspectives on life; and to empower other Parkinson's patients with an honest, sincere and inspirational view on living life positively with a chronic disease.

Tremors in the Universe takes the reader on an intimate journey from sensing something in my universe was wrong, through the decision to start treatments, to PD's effects on my daily life, family and business.

It looks at my choice to participate in the Michael J. Fox Foundations PPMI (Parkinson's Progression Markers Initiative) clinical trial in the hopes of isolating a biomarker that may lead to or contribute toward developing a cure, as well as my devotion and commitment to fundraising on behalf of Parkinson's research.

Simultaneously, the reader can share in and experience the inspirational gift that is my reawakening to my spirituality. By delving deep within my soul, I discover the essence of my strength to establish a life-altering relationship with Parkinson's.

Through the recollections of childhood events and their relationships to shaping my attitudes today, you will discover the connections in life that bind us all together—connections that are far stronger than the Parkinson's that is trying to destroy them.

The thoughts I share regarding my spirituality are not intended to pass judgment on anyone's religion, faith, or belief, or to promote my views. They are simply my thoughts and ideas regarding my spirituality, and an observation of how my spiritual growth is being affected by Parkinson's (and vice versa).

This book is an opportunity for me to share my experience with other Parkinson's patients, both newly diagnosed as well as seasoned professionals. It is also a chance for me to work through my thoughts about both my faith and Parkinson's by writing them down. Most of all, I hope that it paints a meaningful representation for my children of who their father is and what he is about.

Parkinson's disease has many symptoms, stages and degrees of severity, and the physical and emotional challenges vary as well. Therefore, it is extremely important that I acknowledge I am writing from the perspective of an individual who is at the beginning stages of the disease. I cannot profess to know the personal challenges and emotions that individuals in more advanced stages might be experiencing. *Tremors in the Universe* is my personal journal, which serves to document my symptoms, progression and emotional and physical states. My hope is that it might remove some of the mystery of Parkinson's disease for newly diagnosed patients. More importantly, it offers an extremely personal look into the feelings, thoughts and emotions that one person experienced after receiving a diagnosis of a chronic disease, and the first years of adapting and coming to terms with it.

When I began writing, I couldn't help but think that my relationship with Parkinson's and my spiritual beliefs would become more deeply intertwined. My intuition was correct. Each has played a profound role in shaping and altering the course of the other and some very enlightening events have taken place.

This is but one mile on the path of my life.

Acknowledgements

To all who have met me on my path and walked beside me,
your love and friendship helped me realize a passion.

To Jeff, Jerome, Nancy, Patrick, Staci, and Terry:
Thank you for holding pieces of my life's map.
You gave me direction. You changed my life.
I love you all.

To the National Parkinson Foundation:
Thank you for changing my world.

And to Michael J. Fox:
"Our challenges don't define us. Our actions do."
Thank you for everything you have done.

INTRODUCTION
SWIMMING WITH A DOLPHIN

My Parkinson's island is located in the warm waters of the South Pacific. The exact latitude and longitude is 41° 88" North, 87° 63" West, should you ever decide to visit or you have the ability to make an airdrop of rations to me anytime in the near future.

That's right. I live on one of the Parkinson's Islands. They're actually scattered all over the globe. I just happened to land on one of the islands with a beautiful, sunny view. I've lived on my island for almost two-and-a-half years now. At least I think it's been that long. I used to keep track of the days by making a knife cut in the side of one of the palm trees, but after about four months, the tree fell down. Apparently I was making the marks a bit too deep.

That actually worked out for the best, however. I split the palm tree in half, hollowed out the center and placed the two halves on the ground with the troughs facing up. I filled the troughs with coconuts, strapped a palm leaf to each of my feet and I had myself a treadmill for my morning workout.

Hey, you know what they say, "When life gives you lemons, make lemonade, find someone with vodka and have a party."

On my island I am continuously finding reasons to celebrate. The weather is gorgeous. Temperatures tend to hover around a comfortable 80 degrees beneath perfectly blue, sunny skies, and a light trade wind keeps the leaves of the palm trees dancing and singing for me every day.

Spend some time alone on an island and you'll quickly become keenly aware of the kind of harmonious relationship that exists throughout all of life and between all living things. One element affects another, and each benefits from the other as well.

Take, for example, the leaves of the palm tree and the wind. Without the wind caressing the leaves with its touch, the leaves would never dance; and without the outstretched arms of the leaves to grasp at the breeze, the wind would have no voice. The symphony of life is music to be enjoyed, and it plays daily and for free all around us.

But it's how it all works in harmony that mesmerizes me. I've been keenly aware of those connections ever since I was a little boy; however, as often happens when people grow older, they tend to put the carefree qualities of their youth away amongst their other memories and soon they forget how they used to see things. Wonder is replaced by reality, dreams by necessity, and desires by acceptance.

I had truly lost that vision of my youth. I wasn't seeing out of those eyes anymore. I had gone blind to a lot of the beauty that exists in life and a lot of the life that exists in me.

And then I was given an island.

It's only when we retreat to being alone with our thoughts and we are presented with the opportunity to turn inward for solace that we can rediscover the treasures we held onto as a child. I've been fortunate. I once again found my youthful vision, curiosity and playful perspective on life, and rediscovered my awe of all the wonder that surrounds me. I've reconnected to my spirit and my soul, and I've regained the knowledge that the same connection between the wind and the leaves exists between myself and every other living piece of energy. On my island, I am realizing my dreams. I'm swimming with a dolphin. I'm reconnected and I'm fulfilled.

I found myself on this island shortly after being diagnosed with Parkinson's disease in 2012. I think, to some degree, everyone who receives a PD diagnosis (or any chronic disease for that matter), receives an island of his or her own as well. The differences from one island to the next tend to be how the individual chooses to use it. For some, their island is a place to turn away from everyone, to maroon themselves in anger and bitterness, while others use it as an oasis for growth.

I needed my island for introspection. I needed to have time alone with my thoughts to come to terms with what Parkinson's was going to be in my life. I was determined from the beginning to take an active role in my disease. How I felt about it was something that I could control and Parkinson's could not. I knew in my heart I was stronger than PD, although I didn't understand why. But I wanted to know—I needed to know.

So I decided to write.

I chose to journal my experience for three distinct reasons: to come to terms with my feelings; to educate my children about their father; and to share my journey and spiritual beliefs in the hope that they might benefit someone else on their own path.

I can honestly say I've achieved all three.

Over a 6-month period I have written well over fifty letters to myself. I have reached deeper into my soul, my very being, than I ever imagined possible. I discovered that one's essence lies at the bottom of a very deep well. My journey has been painful and euphoric. It has been dark and frightening at times, and it has been equally enlightening and humorous. I have cried over things that I have learned about myself, yet found myself laughing equally hard. I have understood everything, yet realized I have no answers. I've met teachers along the way and discovered I have lessons I can share as well.

The most profound discoveries however, have come to me through metaphors, recounting stories from my youth. The whimsical perspective I had on my world as a child has enabled me to see my Parkinson's positively with a skewed vision today.

The title *Tremors in the Universe* just came to me. It felt right and sounded right, and it couldn't have been more prophetic. Parkinson's has indeed shaken up my world. It's shaken me awake to the universe that is my life and made me aware of the gifts that are all around me. It has shaken me out of a slumber that had disconnected me from my faith, and it has reconnected me to myself, first, and finally to others.

The outwardly radiating rings on the water's surface that appear on the cover were equally instinctual. When I thought "tremor", I thought of how an earthquake sends out a shock wave. Not a wave that destroys, but rather one that causes people to take notice. Nothing more.

Those waves would come to be the metaphor for the most profound aspects of my journey.

In everyone's universe, the individual is at the center. Your thoughts and actions radiate out from you and have the potential to affect everything they touch. That energy you send out will eventually come back to you, and, as such, love needs to be the energy that starts at your center—a love of yourself and a love for the unique and perfect individual you are. Then everything that radiates out from you can come from that center of love. The waves are connected to you, which connect you to everyone else. We all are connected. Always.

My discovery on this journey has been that love is at the core of my very being. The Parkinson's disease that wants to destroy connections has, instead, awakened me to the importance of strengthening my connections to myself and to my universe—the need to be intimately connected through love. The feeling of truly being in touch with people and to life, through open and honest conversation where people demonstrate respect, tolerance, and love, is really all it is about for me.

My Parkinson's island is conveniently located at the center of my universe, and I am sitting in the center of my island underneath a palm tree as the leaves dance in the breeze. As I sit here alone with my thoughts, I write. I write about my experiences, my life, my pains and my joys, and what I've learned. But more importantly, I write about my love for what I know exists outside my island. Even though I can't always hold it, touch it or talk to it, I know its there. I write because I think, *Maybe if I share how my attitude and choices have made a positive difference for me here on my island, someone else might receive that message. And then everything will be ok on their island and they will be the happier for it.*

So with each chapter I wrote, I put my thoughts and my love in a bottle and set it afloat. And like thoughts in the universe, the waves are carrying the bottles over the horizon.

I honestly never considered whether or not anyone would ever discover one of the bottles. In the beginning, it was more a matter of just setting my thoughts adrift. I'd place one in the water and over time it would disappear from my view.

Then a remarkable thing happened: a bottle came back. And a few more!

Some contained very brief notes. Some were filled with heartfelt letters. But they all had made connections nonetheless.

Some were notes and letters from islands I never imagined existed.

Spouses and children of Parkinson's patients told me how they are the ones who have been castaways. Their loved ones never talked to them or shared their experiences with PD, so they felt completely helpless to understand.

I heard from children who lost their parent to Parkinson's disease who expressed how my messages, in some way, lessened the pain for them.

Other letters were from Parkinson's patients, who found inspiration in my positivity, and many were from my close personal friends, the closest waves in my universe that sent airdrops of support and well wishes.

The bottles are now afloat for my children should they want to understand me in greater detail, though I'm hopeful that a lot of what I have expressed in my writing they already knew through my actions and my love for them. But if there were any one message from the bottles I would hope they receive, it is that no matter what life gives you, you have the power of choice to determine for yourself what the experience will be for you. You are the only one who controls your happiness. Choose to be happy.

As for myself, I'm doing great on my island. I've discovered so much already, and yet I still have so much more of the island to explore. Life's an adventure.

Tremors in the Universe is the culmination of all of those letters. And it's time to cast them out to sea. The tide is high and the outgoing current feels strong. I'm putting all my positive thoughts and energies into this one bottle. My hope and my prayer is that it washes ashore where it is truly needed.

I believe it will.

CHAPTER 1

DID YOU FEEL THAT?

In 2008, at the age of forty-eight, I had vowed that within two years I was going to be in the best physical shape of my life. It was a birthday present I wanted to give myself when I turned fifty, and, to me, fifty was going to be big.

I had always had the experience and been of the belief that each decade of my life was better than the previous.

My teens had been carefree and a constant adventure. My friends and connections were everything to me, and I had boundless energy and was always on the go. Those years were also my introduction to the birth of my spirituality or at the very least provided me my first recollection of being spiritually awakened. I read the book *Illusions: The Adventures of a Reluctant Messiah* by Richard Bach, and it stirred something inside me. The questions that I started to ask—not only of my parents and clergy but more importantly, of myself—started the growth process of my spirit that still is an integral part of who I am today.

My twenties represented personal independence and the foundations of my future, which I embraced with a passion. In those short ten years I attended two universities: Southern Illinois, where I majored in aviation to become a pilot (maybe a carryover from *Illusions*); and the University of Illinois in Urbana/Champaign, where I majored in graphic design, which would subsequently become my life's career. I met my wife during this time and, eventually, would open my own design business, which I still run today.

My thirties were anchoring years when I started and built my family and the decade that would give me a new perspective on life and what was important to me. I was blessed with three beautiful children. My business was prospering.

My forties I found to be the years where I felt everything come together. I had found a comfort in my business, and I knew the cycles that it took, like the ever-changing tide of the ocean. There was just a sense of stability. Our children were coming of age where their personalities were really starting to shine, and I just felt as though I really knew who I was. My spiritual beliefs were in full bloom for me, and I took great comfort in how I saw things for myself.

During every one of those decades, I can recall at least one event (often more) where I felt a special connection on a spiritual nature. Events that I saw as reminders or wake-up calls showing me that there is something more at play in my life. On more than one occasion my guardian angels had wanted to ensure that I made it to the next decade.

And now my fifties were approaching.

To provide a little health background, I had always been able to control my weight. I usually tipped the scales around 175-185 pounds, and, with a six-foot tall frame, I was definitely within a comfortable norm, but my diet had always been something I neglected. For me, my ration of fruit came in a Pop-Tart and vegetables were just something that never appealed to me. Having been a small business owner for the last twenty years, my usual routine was to grab a cup of coffee in the morning, skip lunch to keep the workflow going, and then come home in the evening and have my three meals between 6 p.m. and bedtime. Not quite the way the food pyramids were built. My business is graphic design, so my job consists primarily of sitting at a computer unless I have presentations with a client.

So let's just say by forty-eight I had become "soft."

Well, I made a commitment and promise to myself to change my life. I enrolled in a local gym and signed up with a trainer to do things right. During the next two years, I ran on treadmills, worked with weights, crunched my abs, did sets of sit-ups, pull-ups, push-ups, and throw-ups (well, I felt like I wanted to), and endured the ridicule of my trainer, who was a cancer survivor, so she wasn't going to go easy on me. And you know what? It worked. By the time I reached the age of fifty, I was in the best shape of my life. My weight had leveled at 175. I was toned, muscular, and, best of all, off every medication I had been taking for blood pressure and cholesterol. All my numbers were perfect. I was fifty, and I was feeling fantastic. Happy birthday!! I felt that I had been given the answer for maintaining my health—stay on this regimen, eat fewer Pop-Tarts, have a healthy breakfast once in awhile, and eat sensible meals at night—not only will my fifties be the best decade yet, I'll ensure the decades to come.

I decided to stop working out with my trainer and manage myself from this point on. I had learned and adopted a discipline I felt comfortable with, and I was confident I could maintain what I had learned.

Fast-forward a year and a half to the fall of 2011.

My workout routine had become just that—routine. I kept to a consistent workout of aerobic exercise for thirty minutes, abs for another twenty, and finished up with weights for another twenty.

One day, the routine became anything but ordinary. It was a small change, but I had become very in tune with my body, and something didn't feel right. It was the first small ripple in my universe that would soon redefine my life.

I had been running on the treadmill and suddenly my normal gate felt off. My left leg started to feel like it was slightly heavier, and I sensed that I was starting to feel fatigued in that leg. I thought, if I continue at this pace I'm going to trip and fall and land flat on my face on the treadmill. So I reached up and slowed the speed to a more comfortable setting and finished my workout.

The next day I went back with the intent of resuming my original pace simply to discover a repeat of the same sensations. My leg was feeling clumsy. A minor glitch, I thought. Maybe I had tweaked a muscle and my body was just telling me to slow down. I accommodated. For a few weeks I took things slower with the goal of letting things mend.

What transpired over the course of the next nine months, however, was far from recuperating. I was about to start a downward spiral, both physically and mentally, and begin an exhaustive self-guided search through the medical community for answers to what was happening to me.

Also, at a time when I should have been turning to my own spiritual beliefs for comfort and strength, I found my spirit being broke.

~

2011 to this point had already been a tumultuous year, and my stress was gradually mounting. The economy was struggling, and the ripples of that crisis were reaching my business. When a bad economy hits business, advertising, marketing, and design budgets are generally the first to get the axe. I had been through this before in '87 and then later in the '90s, but this time things took on a different flavor. For the first time, I had my accounts coming to me asking me what sacrifices I could make to help strengthen their business. The one position of strength I always held during these periods was the size of my business. I'm a small "boutique" firm and, as such, carry minimal overhead and usually look attractive to companies that are dumping their large firms in the hopes of streamlining budgets. The downside during these times? The size of my business. I was now doing all the work myself, having had to let my only employee go when the economic downturn took hold.

My oldest daughter was in college, and my youngest daughter was finishing her senior year of high school and solidifying her commitment to a university as well. So to say money was top of mind at this time with the thought of two in college in 2012 was an understatement, and our economy just was not cooperating.

I needed to keep one step ahead.

Oh, but wait! That's right. My step seems to be a little bit off.

As I mentioned earlier, around August of 2011 the first sign that something was physically wrong for me was the slowing of my left leg on the treadmill at the gym, but it didn't stop there. About this same time, I started to take notice of additional oddities.

Every so often when walking my left foot would catch on the carpet. Not enough to make me fall, but enough to make me take notice and stumble a bit. Additionally, in my haste to maneuver my way through the house, I would periodically misjudge the corner wall and slam my shoulder into it, jarring me back into a sense of reality.

Now my spiritual side would find humor in this. I could easily imagine a loved one who had passed on getting a chuckle by making me take that off step that drove me into the wall, or their spirit pulling up the carpet just a tad to catch my foot. There are a lot of comedians in my family that have moved on, and it wouldn't have surprised me at all if they were at work behind this. On more than one occasion, I recall myself blurting out loud, "Not funny!" to which I imagined one of them on the other side laughing and saying, "Yeah. It really is!"

But as time went on, I stopped laughing.

By September the stumbles and the miscues started happening with more frequency—not daily, but definitely enough for me to take notice—and along with it new maladies began to emerge. The next was a stiffness that took over my left hand. It felt as though my hand was physically swollen, but to the naked eye nothing was apparent. My fingers were hard to bend and inside them was a general ache. I would use my good right hand to exercise the left, grabbing the fingers and flexing them back and forth, back and forth. Strangely, after going to bed each night, I would wake up in the morning and they would feel much better. I could move them effortlessly, but after a half-day in the office typing at the keyboard, my fingers were as stiff as could be again. Luckily, I am right-handed, so the majority of my design mouse work at the computer is done with my right hand not my left, but my typing was presenting problems.

Next came my left shoulder with an ache in the rotator cuff that was becoming bothersome at night. There wasn't a position I could lay in bed that didn't awaken me from the discomfort. I was still trying to work out with regularity at the gym, mind you, so I thought I hadn't learned everything from the trainer on proper technique as I thought I had. Maybe this was an injury from lifting incorrectly.

At this point, not only had I adjusted speed on the treadmill, but I'd reduced my time devoted to weightlifting as well. I was slowing down.

Yet ironically, just like a car getting up there in miles, the problems seemed to keep coming, one after another, with greater speed: tingling in my left hand down to the fingers; tingling in my left foot. Simultaneously, I started to feel less "grounded" when I walked, a state somewhere between feeling light-headed and dizzy.

Then in October came the wake up call I needed to say, "Enough is enough," and to get myself to my internist.

I had pulled into a McDonalds on my way to work to order a cup of coffee for the commute ahead. As I tried to speak the words I had uttered so many times before, "One large black coffee, please," the words came out a jumble. "Un lah bwa kaaf." I stopped myself and tried again, only to hear the same result come out of my mouth in what sounded like the most alien voice to me.

My heart raced and I composed myself as I tried for the third time to place my order—with success. I honestly was frightened. I pulled over into one of the parking areas and assessed myself to try and judge if I was having a stroke but, for all appearances, I now seemed fine. Sitting alone in my car, I repeated the same order—over and over and over—with no mistakes. All arms work, all legs work, no facial changes. I was fine.

But I was definitely calling my doctor.

By the time I saw my internist I was armed with the list of symptoms I'd amassed, as long as a football coach's playlist. I was experiencing periodic heart palpitations and a trembling feeling every time I used my muscles, quite often in the simplest of ways, like filling the dog bowl with water. The heavier the bowl would get, the more my hand would start to tremble. Stretching when I arose from bed in the morning would send the muscles in my body into a shiver. Simply trying to turn over in bed and resting on one arm would cause the muscles in that arm to shake. The tingling was becoming transient, moving from my left side to my right. I was no longer working out because, by the end of a full day at the office, I was completely exhausted.

There I sat, alone, on the exam table in the doctor's office.

His walls were adorned with the usual brochures, charts and props that explain various diseases. I had actually worked on some medical promotions like this from time to time in my business. I found myself walking his exam room looking at the educational aids, both critiquing the design work and educating myself medically.

What about Hyperthyroidism? It has a lot of my symptoms. They're all listed right here. Multiple sclerosis? Possible, although I'd had an MRI some five years previous during a bout of stress headaches and everything checked out fine. Parkinson's disease? Could be.

After barraging my doctor with my symptoms, I led with just that last prognosis. "What about Parkinson's?"

To which my doctor replied, "Gee, you're sure jumping ahead on this."

I've long been a believer that when it comes to medicine and your individual medical care, you have to be your own advocate. Never in all of my experience would that become truer than now.

The next four months would include a myriad of specialists and tests, which ultimately lead to clarity and resolution.

I hold in my heart that the people we meet and encounter in our lives all serve a purpose. They are part of a greater plan, helping us navigate our way through life. You never know who may hold that next opportunity, special gift or answer for you.

I do know I have many to thank for helping me get the answer I sought.

Chapter 2

Zero Gravity

As I sat in my doctor's office discussing medical possibilities and courses of action, I realized how heavy the weight of the past year was bearing down on me. Not knowing what was wrong had given fuel to anxiety and panic, and my symptoms had compounded themselves. The simultaneous stress related to work was sapping my strength and energies even more, which made dealing with my health a challenge.

I was considering taking on a second job in the evening to supplement my income, which was still taking a hit from the economy. 2011 was drawing to a close, and I recall being anxious for it to come to end so that I could put the year behind me. *2012 simply HAS to be better*, I'd say to myself. It couldn't be any worse.

Little did I know.

My doctor's approach epitomized the scientific method. For those who need a recap of their high school science days, the scientific method goes like this:

- **Ask a question**
- **Do background research**
- **Construct a hypothesis**
- **Test your hypothesis by doing an experiment**
- **Analyze your data and draw a conclusion**
- **Communicate your results**

Now that's all fine and good, until ego becomes a part of the equation and begins to hinder making sound decisions in the best interest of the patient.

Please don't misunderstand. I most definitely know that my doctor had my best interests at heart, but, in my opinion, his primary motivation was to solve everything himself. He saw me as a medical school assignment or challenge and often commented to me that he loved the stories I came in with because I documented my health so well. He was determined to find the answer.

Hypothesis 1: I had a retrovirus within my system from a bout of shingles I'd had two years prior.

I was put on a medication for 3 months with no positive results.

Hypothesis 2: I wasn't sleeping correctly.

In January of 2012, he sent me for a sleep study to determine my quality of sleep. My doctor hypothesized that, if I had sleep apnea, every disturbance in my breathing at night would send my system into a panic for oxygen. This would create an internal system "panic reaction", giving rise to a chemical reaction in my brain that would, in turn, cause physical symptoms to manifest themselves during my daily activities.

Test and conclusion: I most definitely had sleep apnea.

During the course of this overnight sleep study, my breathing stopped 120 times. My blood pressure was measured at 152/120, and my oxygen levels at sleep were 80% (normal is in the 90% range). It was explained to me that I was never getting the beneficial REM sleep that was needed to rejuvenate my body, so during the day I was paying the price. The answer was to simply fit me with a CPAP machine (night breathing mask) and my problems would be over.

I started the CPAP machine and used it as prescribed. My apneas were eliminated and my wakefulness and concentration during the day improved. My doctor started me on a blood pressure medication, which regulated my blood pressure to 120/65. However, I still found myself with shortness of breath, a feeling of it being hard to catch my breath and this constant need to take deep breaths a lot.

With the exception of my wakefulness and concentration, all of my other symptoms were still present.

I was medically treading water.

The symptom of muscle shaking I had experienced earlier became a constant "jitteriness" running throughout my body, a feeling similar to having just walked in from the cold. It wasn't visible on the outside, but if I were to give someone a hug they'd say, "Wow, are you cold? You're shaking inside."

Searching for answers, I slowly began to make adjustments in my life. A change in my diet was my first approach. Attributing the jitteriness to caffeine intake, I eliminated all coffee and sodas—to no avail. I began drinking green teas for their antioxidant benefits. I even turned to a probiotic regimen, thinking I had an imbalance in my gut and that I needed to rebuild my system. Nothing seemed to work and I was becoming more and more frustrated.

My doctor visits were becoming more frequent, and trials with medications equally so. We would try one drug, only to have it exacerbate symptoms, then immediately switch to another until we found some positive results. To my surprise, my doctor had not recommended I see a specialist. Quite to the contrary. On one particular visit, after discussing everything tried to date, he expressed that, without an answer soon, he would likely suggest I see a holistic doctor, as he had run out of answers. And that he hoped he wouldn't see me back in six months, unable to walk.

A change in direction was imminent.

I began sharing my story with friends in hopes that maybe somebody knew of someone who'd had a similar experience. The fact that things were amiss in my life was also becoming very apparent to those I was closest to.

There were those who approached me with tough love and figuratively slapped me upside the head to say, *You're just not like yourself anymore. You're neglecting your work, your positive nature is gone and we're concerned about you. You have to make a change for yourself.*

Then there were others with whom the stories resonated. They *had* known someone close to their hearts that my experiences reminded them of. Their willingness to share and express concern ultimately made a difference, changed a path, opened a door and eventually led me to an answer.

But first I had a few more appointments along the way.

My shortness of breath was becoming one of the most troublesome symptoms to me, probably because it was the most constant. One day, exasperated, I called my internist and said I wanted the name of a cardiologist. I had tingling in my left side, numbness, pain, and shortness of breath, so I surmised a lot of this might be circulatory.

After a thorough stress test and complete overhaul of my circulatory system, the cardiologist gave me a wonderful review. "Your circulatory system is in fantastic shape. Your heart is as healthy as can be." He even went on to say that he felt my blood pressure issues were more a result of anxiety than anything else, and that if I went off my meds, I'd probably see that my blood pressure was fine—assuming I could control my anxiety.

But the cardiologist also went on to ask another question of me. "Have you ever been to a neurologist?"

I answered, "Yes, 5 years ago. I had some MRIs done that all came out fine."

"Well maybe you should see one again."

This time I went online myself. I reviewed a multitude of doctors' profiles and backgrounds to find someone I felt good about. And it was funny how I ultimately made my decision.

I looked at their pictures. I looked at their eyes. I looked at *them*. And I went with my gut and my heart, and I chose a doctor I thought looked kind, caring and compassionate. I would imagine that most people would assume those characteristics of most any doctor given the field of work they have chosen. But this was more about the instinctive level of listening to my intuition, about getting a feeling and going with it. And this time, as most times, my intuition was right.

I went to her office on the day of my appointment. Again, I was back in that exam room, waiting for the doctor to come in. Only when you're in a neurologist's office, there's nowhere near as much to entertain your senses with. It always struck me how this group of doctors had so little at their disposal for diagnostic tools: a scale here; a blood pressure kit over there; and that tuning fork and reflex hammer rounded out the selections. Not much to do here but just wait.

The doctor entered the room and we exchanged smiles and pleasantries, then got down to the business of me retelling my story.

She did the usual neurologist exams. Close your eyes and touch your nose. Push your arms against her hands. Do the same with your legs. Now your feet. Stand up and walk down the hall so they can observe your gate.

Tap your feet. Open and close your fingers. Open and close your hands, etc. We talked about my family history, past tests and medications I was now taking, and then she gave me her assessment.

"You only exhibit one of the four criteria of Parkinson's disease. And as you may know, you have to exhibit two of the criteria in order to be clinically diagnosed. The one clinical symptom you display is a slight slowness of movement on your left side. Additionally, I observed that you have a very decreased rate of blinking which a lot of Parkinson's patients exhibit as a secondary symptom."

She went on to say that approximately twenty-five percent of Parkinson's patients are misdiagnosed and that these symptoms could fall under what they refer to as Parkinsonism-like symptoms. She said they now had a relatively new test available here in the United States that, until recently, was only available in Europe. The test was called a DaTSCAN™, and that by injecting a radioactive isotope into my system and doing a scan similar to an MRI, they could now accurately measure the amount of dopamine in my brain. The amount of dopamine reduction measured can determine, with greater accuracy, whether or not someone has Parkinson's.

"Would you like to have that test?" she asked.

"Absolutely," I said, without hesitation.

The test was easy and painless, but requires a day of your time. You start with a iodine cocktail to block your thyroid from absorbing any of the radioactive isotopes. Then, after about a three-hour wait for it to take effect, you get an IV line put in and an injection of the isotope. From that point on it's very similar to an MRI: lay in the tube with your thoughts and wait.

In all honesty, a positive result was not the answer I thought I was going to receive. I had been in this mouse maze for so long that I just assumed it would be another dead end and that my search would continue.

Approximately two weeks later, the neurologist's office called me and scheduled an appointment for July 12th, 2012, for me to come in and review the results. The doctor hadn't requested that I have my wife come with me, so I again assumed that I wouldn't have a resolution.

On that day I sat there again, alone in her office. This scenario of waiting in doctors' offices had become too commonplace. Eventually she walked in and we again exchanged smiles.

Without hesitation, she sat down and opened a manila folder. After a brief glance, looked me in the eye and said, "Your results came back positive. You have a seventy to seventy-five percent reduction in dopamine. You have Parkinson's."

I had finally found the door out of the maze and, very surprisingly, the weight of the world was lifted off of my shoulders.

CHAPTER 3

BACK TO MY FUTURE

I often wondered what my reaction might be if I was presented with life-altering news regarding my health.

There I sat in my neurologist's office after just being told I have Parkinson's disease. Surprisingly, I felt a calm come over me as if I had been out in the cold for a long period of time and suddenly a good Samaritan had come along and draped a warm blanket around my shoulders. As strange as it sounds, I was actually relieved. I had been chasing my symptoms for so long that I was beginning to question if anything was truly wrong or whether I had become a hypochondriac. Suddenly, I had been validated.

As I sat there, taking stock of the diagnosis and self-analyzing my reaction (or lack thereof) at the same time, my doctor explained my immediate options and the support groups that were available. She then asked if I was interested in starting drug therapy. She outlined the benefits as well as the risks of the drug she was recommending.

"No...no, not just yet," I replied back to her. "I'd like to learn a little bit more about it first and then make my decision, if that's ok?"

"Absolutely," she said.

She went on to explain, in an almost apologetic tone, that there is not currently a cure for Parkinson's disease, that all they are doing is treating the symptoms. She said Parkinson's is a progressive disease with a wide variety of symptoms and characteristics and, as such, they have a variety of medications available to treat the various symptoms associated with the disease's progression. She then did her best to reassure me by telling me how they have made terrific advances since our grandparents' era, and are continually making new progress.

I acknowledged that I understood and that I appreciated her help in providing me with an answer. We took care of the formalities of exchanging numbers so that I could stay in touch and let her know what my decision was after I had had the time to do some research. She gave me a bag full of informational materials that gave the appearance I had just enrolled in a new course in college.

I guess I had. I was now in a fraternity/sorority with four million members worldwide, one million of those in the United States.

It was time to do my homework.

~

One of my first recollections of a spirit or guardian angel coming to my aid was when I was very young, around six or seven years old. My mom, my brother and I and some neighbors had gone to a public beach one July summer day, and my brother and I were enjoying the water. About fifty yards out from the beach was a wooden raft that a number of the kids would congregate on. If you were a good swimmer, you would jump off the far side of the raft into the deep water. If you were not a good swimmer or simply uncomfortable, you'd stay on the inland side of the raft where the water was shallow.

My only brother is four years older than me and was already a proficient swimmer. I, on the other hand, was not a good swimmer. I hated the swimming lessons I was being sent to regularly because the water at Maple Hill pool where we took instruction was freezing all the time and I never wanted to get in the water. As soon as I would jump in, my chest would tighten from the cold and I couldn't breathe. I'd struggle to catch my breath. But today at the beach, the water was warm and I wanted to be with my brother and his friends, as little brothers often do.

As I made my way out to the raft, I was not swimming. I was jumping as if on a pogo stick. My feet would hit the bottom sand of the lake and I would push off hard to make sure my head stayed above the water. I bobbed up and down like a porpoise the entire way out until my hands reached the raft and my grip assured my safety. I pulled myself up on the raft to enjoy the camaraderie of the other kids in the sun.

Now I'm honestly not clear if it was the rocking of the raft on its floats due to the kids on it that made me lose my balance, or whether I was bumped or pushed, but nevertheless, I quickly found myself in the water on the wrong side of the raft.

I remember as I was transitioning from the solid footing of the raft to being suspended in the air over the lake below, taking a large breath of air to fill my lungs because I knew I was about to go down. I pierced the water and felt a shock of terror wash over my body as my feet and arms flailed and my body slowly sank into the depths. It seemed like an eternity before my feet hit the bottom. I pushed off hard to catapult myself upward toward the glistening surface of the lake that I saw above me. My head and shoulders cut through the surface into the warm air above and, as quickly as I could, I let out a scream to announce my predicament. Exhaling the previous air I had taken in, I quickly followed it with another gasp to inhale as much air as possible, because I was going down again. On the second time down I felt a weakness take over, and my push off of the bottom didn't feel as efficient. But I managed to get my mouth and nose just above water so I could refill one more time.

The third descent gave the sensation of slowing time altogether. My body was floating slowly downward to the lake bottom, and everything was so eerily quiet; however, my feet eventually reached the bottom and with some determination, I pushed off again. This time, as I peered up towards the light, I could tell that my face was not going to break the water's surface.

But my hand did.

As my hand broke the surface of the water, it was met by the grip of another. In one swift motion, I was pulled from the water like a fisherman retrieving his catch. My savior was no one I knew, a man of maybe twenty years of age. He carried me back to shore and put me on solid ground.

For a brief moment in time, I had lost my balance. I found myself in unfamiliar territory where I didn't have the skill or knowledge to help myself. The harder I struggled, the deeper I sank, and over time I began to lose my energy and my ability to catch my breath and focus. Ultimately, it was a willingness to keep trying that brought me to the hand of someone who restored my balance and kept me from drowning.

Back on solid ground in my neurologist's office, I gathered my things and made my way out to my car. It was a warm and sunny day in July.

Now my wife was aware of my appointment that day and had asked me if I wanted her with me, to which I answered no, as I really didn't think it necessary and the doctor hadn't implied any need. Again, I truly didn't anticipate receiving a positive result. But she had insisted that I call her as soon as I was done with the appointment to share the results.

So with the same candor and matter-of-fact approach my doctor had just used, I called and simply said to my wife, "I got the results and they're positive. I have Parkinson's." I reassured her that I was truly doing fine with it and that I had this remarkable sense of relief. I remember saying to her that one of my predominant thoughts was, "This could have been so much worse." To me, I was being given the opportunity to see my children grow older, marry, have families of their own and participate in their lives. My symptoms I had been dealing with for so long to this point very easily could have had another more grave outcome or diagnosis that didn't hold as much opportunity. I really tried to think of myself as blessed—which I still do to this day.

Just think of the number of people who have lived with this disease, I thought to myself. Muhammad Ali and Michael J. Fox immediately came to mind. Each has been living with it for well over twenty years. *If I can get another twenty to thirty years from my body, that will put me in my eighties.* The thought was reassuring.

I quickly came to the decision that now was not the time I wanted to share the diagnosis with our children, though. Our oldest and youngest daughters were each going off to college in just a few short weeks. I didn't want them worrying about me, but instead wanted them each to enjoy their own experience at college—my oldest daughter, her last year, and my youngest daughter, her first year. Somehow sending them off with, "Your dad has Parkinson's. Have a great year at college!" just didn't seem right. To this point, I had never complained about any of my symptoms or even made them aware of them. I had pretty much been fighting my own private battle all along. It was really only my wife and close friends who truly knew what I was dealing with. My parents and the rest of my family would have to wait as well, for reasons I will detail later.

Interestingly for me, my wife and my children were my biggest concern when it came to my diagnosis. It wasn't about me or about how I would handle this disease. How I would manage it was in my hands and I felt confident I could deal with whatever challenges it brought me.

What I couldn't bear to think about was being a burden to my family in the future. I didn't want them to resent me for how this disease may change *their* lives. I was determined put on a strong face and show my children that Parkinson's would not define me.

It was still very early in the day after my appointment, so I drove to the office thinking I could still get in some good work. As I sat down at the computer armed with this new revelation about my life I did what most people would do. I went on the Internet.

Prior to this point in time I had tried to stay off the internet and resist researching my symptoms as much as possible because, as most people know, when you start to do that you can quickly learn that, with just sniffles and a sneeze, the information on the internet will have you dead within three weeks.

But there I sat, looking at my reflection in the monitor, while typing "Parkinson's disease" in the Google search window. *Is this who I am now?*

Return.

What permeated the screen was a list of medical reference sites like WebMD, the Mayo Clinic, and other medical facilities specializing in Parkinson's treatment, support groups and foundations. Of all the sites listed on the page, one in particular caught my attention: The Michael J. Fox Foundation for Parkinson's Research, a name that goes with that friendly warm face of the actor everyone my age knows and loves.

I clicked on the link and the site filled my screen. I admit, the designer in me couldn't help but take notice of how inviting, friendly and well-designed the site looked. (Designers are cursed with always being keenly aware of the appearance of things in our world. For example, I often times will sit down at a dinner table and find myself unconsciously placing my glass in the very center of my napkin, or moving something to the center of a tile on the countertop because it fits better in the grid I see in my mind's eye. It's appreciating visual order.)

A colorful logo of a running orange fox with a long bushy tail adorns the masthead of the page. There's a great picture of Michael looking healthy and happy with that characteristic gleam in his eye and warm smile. Various headlines and subheads vie for your attention: "Donate." "Fundraise." "Participate." But it was the sub-head, "Recently Diagnosed with Parkinson's and Not Taking Medicines Yet? We'd Like You to Participate in a Clinical Study" that caught my attention.

I clicked on the story and read on.

"The Parkinson's Progression Markers Initiative (PPMI) is a landmark clinical study to better understand the progression of Parkinson's disease (PD). The goal of PPMI is to identify and assess biomarkers, objective measures of Parkinson's disease in people who have PD, people who do not have PD and groups of people who may be at risk to develop PD."

It went on to explain that this global initiative study was looking to enroll four hundred recently diagnosed PD patients worldwide (yes, worldwide!) and just forty patients in the United States. To me, those numbers were so small, and yet it appeared that they were still aggressively searching for patients to enroll.

As I studied the article in greater depth, I learned that one of the locations where the study was being conducted was right in Chicago at the Northwestern Medical Faculty Foundation and was being directed by one of the leading neurologists in the country.

The thought of being an active participant in my disease was far better than being passive and waiting to see what the disease was going to do to me.

I thought of my diagnosing doctor and her statement that there is nothing presently you can do for the disease to stop its progression. "We can only treat the symptoms." Suddenly to me there was the possibility that I *could* do something about it. I could get involved.

I called the number listed and spoke to the clinical director. They were most anxious to meet with me—and I was most anxious to meet with them.

Power up the flux capacitor; I had a date with my future.

CHAPTER 4

180°

Now for the sake of full disclosure, my upcoming appointment in August of 2012 with the Northwestern Medical Faculty Foundation and the Michael J. Fox Foundation regarding the PPMI clinical study was not entirely an altruistic act on my part. I most definitely recognized the positive psychological benefit that participation offered me to be taking an active role in my disease. I sincerely liked the idea of contributing my time and, in essence, my body to helping researchers in their goal of establishing a statistical biomarker that may ultimately lead to a cure for Parkinson's disease. But I also saw something more practical and medically prudent in addition to all of that.

Keep in mind I am a small business owner, and with today's rising healthcare costs, in order to make things as affordable as possible for a family of five, I carry quite a high medical insurance deductible on each of us. The DaTSCAN™ alone that I just had done to reach my diagnosis had cost well into the thousands of dollars to finally acquire an answer, not to mention the previous nine months' worth of blood tests, specialist appointments, scans and medications. Combined with a slowdown in the economy and my own business, these had put quite a strain on my financial resources.

My diagnosing doctor had just informed me that Parkinson's disease is misdiagnosed twenty-five percent of the time. My online research confirmed that figure. However, the relatively new test I had done provided greater accuracy of diagnosis, which was not used in the previous statistical data.

Still, it naturally goes without saying that initially there was some thought on my part that maybe I was one of those statistics, and that my diagnosis might be incorrect.

In my research regarding the foundation's PPMI study, I realized that by meeting with them and presenting them with my diagnosing doctors results, they were still going to want to repeat all of the same tests along with a few of their own to verify the diagnosis and validate my participation in the study. They needed to know I had Parkinson's under their criteria. There would be a repeat of the DaTSCAN™, blood tests, urinalysis, cognitive tests, neurological exam, etc., all provided through the foundation.

In essence, I was going to be getting my second opinion from the best doctors and facility in the area at no cost to me. If the results came back positive again, then it was a win-win situation. The foundation would most definitely have received the commitment of another patient for the study, and I felt I would have the best doctors, facilities and care overseeing the progress of my disease, while having access to the most cutting edge research.

My date with the foundation and Northwestern doctors was now set for the 24th of August 2012. Although my appointment was just a few short weeks away, it seemed like forever because I was anxious to get started. They asked me to bring copies of my previous tests results with me, which required a few days for me to chase down.

My initial screening required eight hours and was spread out over two days. After the screening and repeat of the DaTSCAN™, I would be notified within ten to fourteen days of the results and their interest in having me participate.

In the meantime, it was interesting what began to happen to some of my previous symptoms that had brought me to this point. The tingling in my hands and feet, along with the numbness and shortness of breath, slowly began to subside. It was as if that same blanket of calm that had been veiled over me was now soaking deep within me and washing away some of the symptoms. What I came to realize was that a great deal of what had been happening to me was anxiety and stress doing a major number on my body. The "not knowing" was causing me to create more problems for myself than were actually medically warranted. A change in my thought pattern turned out to be a cure for some of what ailed me.

I had also taken it upon myself to seek the assistance of a bone & joint doctor and had received some cortisone shots for my aching shoulder that offered relief for months at a time. The predominant symptoms that remained were: the sense of not feeling grounded when I walked; a weakness of my left extremities; a slowness of motor skills with my left hand; the periodic stumbles, balance issues, misjudgments of space; and the underlying jitteriness that still ran through my body. But the Inderal I was now on regularly for blood pressure was managing that.

Over the next week, I would receive periodic emails containing consent forms and authorizations to review and sign to bring to my initial exam. I also received literature outlining the study's schedule of activities and what the participation goals were. If eligible, I would be asked to return in forty-five days for a baseline visit. During this additional eight-hour appointment, some standard testing would be repeated, such as blood pressure, temperature, weight and general health questions, along with some new neurological exams, cognitive testing, blood and urine testing, an MRI, and lumbar puncture/spinal tap to collect cerebral fluid for storage and research tests.

Once all of the baseline procedures had been completed, I would then be enrolled in the study. I would agree to return every three months for the first year, and then every six months for the next four years, for a complete study of five years.

The days before my appointment were filled with lots to do, so the time actually went by pretty fast. My eldest was already at college and we had my youngest daughter to move to school as well. As I said my goodbyes to my two daughters, I found myself wondering about how quickly Parkinson's could progress. In all likelihood I wasn't going to be seeing them until their Thanksgiving break and I wondered if, at that time, they would see a drastic difference in their dad.

Only time would tell.

August 24, 2012. The day of my screening had finally arrived. My appointment was for 8:00am, so I had to get an early start. The one-hour drive downtown from our home in the Chicago suburbs would give me ample time alone with my thoughts.

I love driving. I always have. My family would always joke about how I should have been a cab driver; because when I would get to the city I would drive with total abandon. In my weak attempt at fatherly wisdom, I would say, "You have to drive like a cabbie, like you belong here, otherwise you're just in the way," all the while zipping in and out of traffic. My stick shift usually made it all the more adventurous, my wife holding onto the handrail overhead and my children in the back seat giggling.

~

My second recollection of feeling there was something special at play in my universe came during my first year of college at Southern Illinois University in Carbondale, Illinois. I was an aviation major and following my dream of becoming an airline pilot. The classes were divided into two curriculums: Airframe and Power Plant Mechanic License and Flight School.

The A&P curriculum would provide me with the license to fix any aircraft in the world, from a single engine Piper Cub to a Boeing 747. I knew I would never use this part of my degree because I had already come to the conclusion that I didn't want to be responsible for the lives of five-hundred-some people on an airline, with my name signed off on the repair log book.

The other half of my major was flying. There I was at peace: a day spent amongst the clouds and alone with my thoughts, observing the world from an entirely different perspective, everything so small yet obviously all connected. The farm fields formed grids down below. Everything definitely had order.

As a student in aviation, the vast majority of classes were off campus at the airport and, as such, meant that as a freshman you could have your own car on campus for the drive to and from the airport.

I had worked every summer during high school and had always managed to save enough to have a car to drive. My very first car at the age of sixteen was a Mazda wagon, stick shift, the car that had the goofy commercial for the Mazda Wankel rotary engine. They had a funky jingle that went something like, "Piston engine goes boing, boing, boing, but the Mazda goes hum." I loved that commercial.

But as I prepared to go off to college, I wanted a new car. I went to the Hertz auto rental company because they sold used cars from their rental fleet. The cars were usually only one or two years old at the most. It was there I found my next car, a 1976 silver Chevy Camaro. Oh, how I loved that car. It was perfect for an 18-year-old and a wonderful ride for those drives from campus out to the airport in southern Illinois.

That area of southern Illinois is beautiful, with vast open spaces and rolling hills dotting the area, a rarity in the usually flat landscape of the state. The sprawling roads, which weaved through farmland with rarely a stop sign, offered a perfect opportunity to open the throttle of my Camaro and enjoy the ride.

Well, there was one day in particular that I remember. After completing my hours in the air for the day, I hopped in my car to make the drive back to campus from the airport. The day was sunny and clear. Visibility was perfect and so was my vision. I was going to be a pilot after all; I prided myself on my 20/20 vision.

Now this route that I took happened to be one of those characteristically flat areas of Illinois. For those of you who have not been to our state, it's the kind of area that, as long as the corn isn't too tall, you can see a cow on the horizon and nothing in between. Freshly plowed farm fields surrounded me. So, from my vantage point, I could see everything for miles around me just as if I were still up in the air. The stretch of open road I was presently on was as straight as could be, with a stoplight visible about two miles ahead, a road that dissecting the intersection from left to right. My speed? Probably seventy miles per hour.

As I continued on, a sparkle of light caught my eye to my left. I glanced to the left and saw a car approaching on the road that would intersect my path at the stoplight ahead. The sun was reflecting off his chrome side mirrors like a lighthouse beacon in the night that kept sending out a signal. I looked back toward the stoplight, now about a mile ahead, which had just turned green for me. I kept my speed.

I watched the other car now with growing interest and judged its speed as about equal to mine. The skills I had learned for planning trips by air using maps of the ground, and charting courses with protractors and rulers, were suddenly in my head, measuring perceived distances and estimates of speed. I quickly came to the conclusion that we would both be getting to the intersection at exactly the same time.

But it's a clear day, I thought to myself. *Surely he can see the red light.*
One hundred yards.

My eyes are now rapidly scanning back and forth between his car and the light, and the intersection is closing in fast. *Approaching car. My light is green. He's still coming. Still green. Certainly he's going to start slowing. Green. I'm committing to go. Green.*

As the front of my car entered the intersection I looked one more time to my left. He was not stopping. He was coming through. My leg was instinctively hitting the brake as hard as it could, like you do when you're flying and you want to move the rudder to change the direction of the airplane. I watched as his front bumper approached my door. I remember how clearly I saw the details of his car. And as my mind sent a message to every inch of my body to say, "Now! The impact is going to be now! Brace yourself!!!", my car suddenly changed direction.

Without my turning the steering wheel, at a point when the space between the cars had to be less than an inch, my car moved. It moved as if the air that was being compressed between his bumper and my door was strong enough to move a car. It spun to the right like a matador with his cape allowing the bull to pass.

The bull never stopped.

As quickly as his car had entered the intersection, it was gone again. My car had done a complete one hundred and eighty degree spin, now facing the direction I had just come from, and the other car was gone. I sat there briefly to catch my breath and take in my surroundings. There was no one visible out here at all. I kept thinking, had something happened, there would have been no one to help until someone happened to come along and stumble upon the scene.

I got out of my car and surveyed it on all sides. Not a scratch.

Someone or something was watching over me. Some energy in the universe was helping me.

~

Thankfully, the car ride downtown to Northwestern Medical Center was uneventful, and I was now sitting in the reception area of the twentieth floor of the Galter Pavilion. This is the floor where they work with individuals with a wide range of neurological issues.

It was a strange feeling as I sat there the first time and took in my surroundings. I was now part of this new group, and suddenly I found myself observing other PD patients in the waiting room as if I were looking at myself, sometime in the future. One gentleman had a very visible tremor in his hand. Another had the blank, expressionless "mask" to his face that I had read about in descriptions of various Parkinsonian symptoms. Some patients were delivered in wheelchairs by a spouse or a caregiver.

And here sat me, actually feeling somewhat guilty because, for all outward appearances, I looked to be what most would consider "normal".

Sitting there in that waiting room brought all of the symptoms out of the books and reference materials and transposed them from printed words into living specimens. Human beings.

I was filled with empathy. But do they want me to feel sorry for them?

I certainly didn't, nor do I now, want people to define me or ever feel sorry for me because of Parkinson's. But at the time, I couldn't help but feel something when eyes meet eyes. There's always that connection, always that energy.

"Robert?" I heard my name called.

I looked up and saw the smile of a young, attractive girl wearing a white lab coat, who greeted me with a handshake and an introduction.

"Hi Robert, I'm Christina. I am the research study coordinator and I will be handling most of your screening today and going over our procedures for the study. Are you ready to get started?" she said.

"Absolutely."

CHAPTER 5

X MARKS THE SPOT

If you were to ask me if the universe were associated with human qualities of male or female, I'd feel pretty confident in saying that the universe had double X chromosomes. After all, the universe is a perfect system that gives birth to new stars and galaxies, and nurtures everything within its infinite embrace. It is patient, sustaining and forgiving. I see my universe as an energy that is compassionate, listens and responds.

We reside on Mother Earth. The Universe has to be the Grandmother.

I've always communicated and connected easily with the female sex. A connection on the spiritual level especially. I think that comes from the fact that women are more comfortable openly expressing their feelings and emotions than men. I do have a few male friends that I can discuss spirituality with, but they are fewer and farther between. I like to open up and speak from my heart, so I think it's only natural that I communicate easier with women.

I think a big part of that comes from the fantastic relationship and dialogue I had with my own mother while growing up. I felt comfortable discussing anything with my mom; there wasn't a subject that was off-limits. More importantly, from my mom I learned empathy, kindness and gratitude, and it came to be something I looked for in the relationships I made. I learned how to connect with people on a level that comes from the heart. My dad taught me independence and the importance of hard work, which gave me the courage to start my own business. But my mom gave me the skills to make those business relationships connections of substance that would flourish.

Most women possess an undeniably high level of compassion, which had become an important factor to me in approaching my health care. I had recently cut ties with my male internist of over twelve years because of the way my diagnosis had come about, and I was now actively looking for a female internist to replace him. In my mind, I felt I would receive more compassionate care. It certainly couldn't hurt to try.

So you can imagine my delight when I learned that the staff that would be supporting Dr. Tatyana Simuni, the female neurologist and principal investigator of the clinical study at Northwestern Medical Faculty Foundation were named Christina, Karen and Melanie.

Christina walked me back to a small exam room where the screening process and the bulk of future appointments would take place. The room had an exam table, two chairs and a desk with a computer. The room was actually smaller than the dorm room I had just moved my youngest daughter into.

Christina was barely older than my oldest daughter who was now twenty-one, and I gathered from our conversation that she had recently graduated from Knox College with a Bachelor of Arts degree in psychology. She had found her way to this Parkinson's Progression Markers Initiative through her continuing studies with Northwestern University. She explained that her role was to manage the retention of patients, and oversee procedures and tests for the Chicago location of this 200- million-dollar project that was being funded by the Michael J. Fox Foundation. She openly acknowledged that she had no special connection with Michael because she was too young to have seen any of his TV shows, and she never took interest in his movies.

Oh how my age came crashing home.

We proceeded to go through the initial screening which started with a series of questions that Christina would read from numerous pages that were three-ring-bound into a large white folder. On the front of the folder and on every page was my case number, which she explained to me, had been assigned to me to provide total anonymity throughout the study.

Medical and family history was the first thing we reviewed. Questions ranged from the ordinary to the specific, and throughout the entire process I was fielding my own questions, as well. There was a volley of information going back and forth. From this first visit I learned that, interestingly,

Parkinson's is not a hereditary disease. It's not something you pass down from parent to sibling. They definitely were interested in family history, but because both of my grandfathers had passed away well before I was born (and at relatively young ages), these questions were difficult for me to answer.

We then went through a series of questions to measure my thinking, memory, moods and behaviors. Of all the parts of the initial screening—and future appointments for that matter—this was the bit I liked the least. The questions would challenge even the best of thinkers. It was like a third grader being put in front of the class at the chalkboard and being asked to solve the Pythagorean theorem. It's a setup for embarrassment.

Maybe I could ask to go to the bathroom.

"I'm going to recite a list of ten words for you, Robert," Christina would say. "Try and remember as many as you can. Later, I'm going to ask you to recall as many of those words as possible. Ready?"

"Seven words?" I asked, jokingly.

"No, ten words," she said, not catching my loosely veiled attempt at humor.

"Just kidding," I said. "I'm ready."

"Rose. Hammer. Yellow. Vegetable. Kite. Fluffy. Vodka. Camel. Circle. Mustache," she recited.

Are you kidding me? was my predominant thought. Probably not a good thought either, since I was supposed to be concentrating.

Maybe what they'll really discover is that I'm ADD.

Did she say "vodka"?

We were already on to the next series of questions and tests.

"I'm going to recite letters of the alphabet, Robert, and every time you hear the letter "A", I want you to tap the table. Ok?" Christina recited from the big white book and then glanced at me with a smile.

Really? I thought. "Sure," I responded.

She recited and I tapped.

The battery of questions continued. "Are you depressed?" "Do you find purpose in your life?" "Have you ever smoked?" "Find the giraffe in this picture." "Connect the dots in this drawing." "What word does not fit in the list of words I am about to read to you?" "Do you have any compulsive behaviors?" "What does this picture remind you of?"

We were filling that white book. She was learning everything she needed to know about me and I was learning something, too.

I was going crazy.

"One more question before Doctor Simuni comes in, Robert," she said as she turned the page.

"How many words in the list of ten can you recall?"

"Vodka," I replied with a chuckle.

And then proceeded to riddle off nine more words.

I did it. I put down the chalk and took my seat.

There was a brief knock at the door. It opened slowly and in walked a woman I would guess to be in her forties. (I've never been good at guessing a woman's age so I have learned to always err on the younger side—much better for your health.) I recognized her immediately because I had done my homework. It was Dr. Tatyana Simuni, the principal investigator of this study. As a small business owner and designer, I always researched the company and the individuals I was going to be meeting with. It made good business sense to be prepared. So I already knew of her background and had even read some of her papers on Parkinson's disease. She was an incredibly intelligent doctor and was at the forefront of current research.

She walked in, introduced herself, shook my hand and sat down at the desk that Christina had just gotten up from. She opened my white folder, looked me in the eye and asked, "So, how are you today Robert?" in this wonderful Russian accent.

Ah, that connection! Things were going to be good.

We briefly reviewed all my diagnosing doctor's results before Dr. Simuni conducted an exam for herself: physical exam, neurological exam and a review of my general health and medications, very similar to what had already brought me to this point. And then I told her my story, a recap of the onset and progression of symptoms.

She also shared a story—one about Parkinson's. I quickly realized that what she was really doing was telling me what MY story might become.

Dr. Simuni explained that the progression of Parkinson's was not going to be like falling off of a cliff. I was not going to have one symptom one day, and wake up the next and have drastically more severe case. Parkinson's disease progresses and evolves over time. It comes with a myriad of symptoms. You may get one or two of them, or you may get many of them; there is no way to know for sure. "At present, Parkinson's has no cure. We simply treat your symptoms."

She went on to relate the importance of the work they are doing and, in particular, the landmark status of the PPMI study. Of the forty patients they hoped to enroll in the United States program, close to half of them were participating in the Northwestern study, here in Chicago. If my diagnosis was confirmed and I wanted to partake in the study, I would be one of a very select few that would play an important role in this study.

~

Having an opportunity to do something that can benefit the lives of others wasn't foreign to me. I had been given that gift once before in my life at the age of thirty. Those who are familiar with this time in my life say what a wonderful thing it was that I did. But the true sacrifice that was made at that time was not mine; a five-year-old girl made it. It's incredibly important to me, to this day, to acknowledge her place in this universe. Her life and energy did so much in so few years.

It was 1985. I was coming out of a grocery store in our hometown. As you exit the store with your cart, there is an area where people post flyers ranging from garage sale notices to lost pet postings to teenagers looking for babysitting opportunities. Amongst the colorful paper flyers was one that happened to catch my eye. It was a notice of a blood drive being held in a nearby town for a five-year-old girl who was battling leukemia. It had a picture of this little girl with the most wonderful smile and eyes that sparkled like sunshine.

The drive, sponsored by the National Bone Marrow Registry, was recruiting volunteers to donate a vial of blood for testing in the hope of finding a match for this little girl. I wrote down the date and the address. I had long been a donor of both whole blood and apheresis so giving one more vial was nothing.

I stopped by the donation site on the day of their drive and made my blood donation, along with a cash donation to the family to help them with medical costs. I wished them the best of luck and went on my way.

Over the next five years, the memory of that donation faded except for the periodic letter I would get from the bone marrow registry asking me to verify that my contact information was still the same.

A week before my thirtieth birthday, and just a day before we had planned to leave for Las Vegas to celebrate it with another couple whose husband shared the same birthday, a similar, nondescript letter arrived from the National Bone Marrow Registry. Nothing of significance or importance adorned the envelope. It hadn't been sent by registered mail. For all intents and purposes, I could have very easily assumed that it was the standard verification of address letter I had so often received, and I could have thrown it away unopened. But I opened it.

Inside was a letter that explained that my blood donation and information on the registry had come up as a possible match. It said there were still lots of tests that would need to be done, and that the statistical chances were one in six million that it would ultimately match, but that if I was seriously interested in pursuing tests further, I should contact them at my earliest convenience.

I was reading this on a Friday evening after 5pm. Everyone working at the registry had already gone home, so I left a message expressing that, without hesitation, I was one hundred percent on board.

What transpired over the next sixteen weeks' worth of tests, blood draws, physicals and personal interviews, ultimately led to my being found to be a perfect match for a fifty-three-year-old gentleman in Austria who had leukemia and needed a marrow transfusion.

All along the way, the people at the registry and others familiar with the situation kept saying what a wonderful thing I was doing. Yet, in my mind, I never thought twice about it. I only wondered, *How could ANYONE, given the opportunity to possibly help save another, not do it?*

Even more importantly was another thought at the center of my heart.

On the day of my donation, with doctors and nurses all gathering my information and a man sitting there with his satchel looking like Indiana Jones waiting to take my donation to Austria, the question in my heart came forward.

"I know everyone keeps saying what a wonderful thing this is that I am doing and everyone keeps thanking me, but I'm really not the one who should be thanked," I explained. "There was a little five-year-old girl that had leukemia. I saw a flyer and I made a donation to try and help her. Does anyone know anything about that little girl?"

To which one nurse replied, "Yes. I knew that little girl and she passed away."

"*She* is the one that made this possible," I said with tears coming to my eyes. "She is the one that made the sacrifice that is helping this man in Austria. She is the one that deserves the thanks."

That moment in time, that gift of opportunity I was given, solidified my belief that, in my universe, we are all connected. Every person we meet holds a potential gift for us. In tragedy can come good. And when the opportunity is put in front of us to help someone else, we must. I will forever be connected to that little five-year-old girl.

~

Back at Northwestern, the rest of the initial screening tests for Parkinson's were completed over the course of the day. Within fourteen days, I received confirmation that, yes, I indeed had Parkinson's, and they would like me to become part of the study.

I gave them my acceptance and we scheduled my next appointment for forty-five days out to gather the baseline data that would become part of my ever-growing white folder.

In my mind, I had beat the odds, won the lottery and been given a rare gift and opportunity once again.

CHAPTER 6

THE CENTER OF MY UNIVERSE SMELLS LIKE STRAWBERRIES

My baseline appointment for the Michael J. Fox Foundation PPMI study arrived in October, so I took the day off to drive downtown to Northwestern Memorial Hospital. Never knowing how traffic might be in Chicago on any given day, I had left extra early and ended up arriving a good thirty minutes prior to my appointment. Before heading up to the twentieth floor, I grabbed a cup of coffee and sat down on a couch in the main floor lobby to people-watch.

If you've never been to Northwestern Memorial Hospital (and I hope you never do have to go), it is an impressive place: a state-of-the-art facility that is nationally ranked in sixteen specialties. Of all those, it holds its highest ranking in neurology. The hospital is teeming with doctors, both young and old, and a sense of the incredible knowledge base that exists within its walls is simply awe-inspiring.

What is even more remarkable to observe, is the strength and courage of the patients who visit this facility. You can't help but feel your own situation or problems minimized when you witness the challenges that others are facing.

My appointment was to be very similar to my initial screening except for the addition of a smell test, an MRI, and the lumbar puncture or spinal tap to collect cerebral fluids for research. I had heard stories about spinal taps but never had cause to experience one. I have never been afraid of needles and also have a rather high pain tolerance, so I really wasn't feeling too anxious.

Once I arrived on the twentieth floor I was greeted by Christina, who escorted me back to the exam room. She repeated a number of the standard interview questions we had done during the initial screening. My white folder was getting thicker and thicker, and this was just appointment two.

"Ok, Robert, I now need to test your sense of smell," Christina said as she pulled out a sealed packet. Splitting the ends, she pulled apart the wrapping to remove a booklet of "scratch n' sniffs". *Now this*, I thought, *could be fun*. I was asked to scratch each one individually and, picking from a list of printed names next to it like lemon, cherry, cinnamon, etc., tell Christina the one I thought it smelled like. *Simple.*

The only problem was, I kept telling Christina, "I think you have a faulty packet here. These hardly smell like anything or are so similar I can't tell them apart."

To which Christina replied, "Just do your best."

It turns out that, through the Michael J. Fox Foundation research, tests of this nature have lead researchers to believe that well before conventional symptoms of Parkinson's begin to appear, Parkinson's patients show a decreased sense of smell. I suddenly recalled the numerous times my family would remark, as we drove by a dead skunk on the road, how incredibly foul it smelled, to which I would usually reply, "Oh, its really not *that* bad." And to me, it wasn't.

I'm definitely learning as I go along in this process that there are numerous complexities associated with Parkinson's. I blink far less than the standard person and apparently I have a reduced sense of smell.

I read a quote by Michael J. Fox once where he described Parkinson's as "the gift that keeps taking."

I was beginning to understand.

As soon as Christina had finished our "aroma therapy" session, Melanie came in to take my blood. Melanie is the RN on staff who gathers all the blood samples and is my medication expert as well. She is another fantastic soul among these four incredible women. Melanie's a spunky woman and she and I get along best of all because she just has a great sense of humor.

Melanie's stay was brief, but she gave me the heads up on what to expect with my spinal tap later that afternoon. The most important thing to avoid a headache afterward, she told me, was to take advantage of the time after it to lie down.

Upon Melanie's departure, Dr. Simuni walked in. She briefly reviewed my results from the screening and concurred one hundred percent with my diagnosing doctor. She went on to say how well I must know my body, because most Parkinson's patients would not have picked up on the symptoms quite so early. We briefly discussed my present symptoms, which I described as becoming "slightly more apparent" to me in terms of my slowness of movement. She asked me how I felt about them and was it causing me any distress? To which I replied that, all in all, my attitude's very good.

As she was wrapping things up and was about to leave, I interrupted her with one more question.

"I realize that you wear two hats here, Dr. Simuni. You're the principal investigator for the PPMI study, but you're also a neurologist with a regular practice and patients."

She nodded as she listened, and I continued.

"I need to know, when my condition changes down the road, who can I expect to be with me? Will you be the principal investigator who sees me as a part of this research study? Or will you be the doctor who has a Parkinson's patient?" I paused momentarily and then further explained, "I guess what I am asking is, if I could benefit from medicine or treatment outside of the scope of this study, will you tell me?"

"That's a fair question, Robert," she said. "You can always count on me being a doctor first. I will always have your best interests at heart."

"Will you be my doctor when we are done with this study in five years?" I asked.

"If you want me to be, I will be happy to be," she replied. We smiled at each other and shook hands and she excused herself as Christina returned to escort me to my MRI and spinal tap.

I have had MRIs done numerous times before in my life, so it was nothing out of the ordinary. I'm not claustrophobic, so I actually find them relaxing and an opportunity to catch up on some sleep. I often find myself tapping along with those bizarre rhythms the magnets make, or see if I can come up with a song to hum along with it, all the while wondering why with all the advances in science and technology, they still can't make those machines less noisy.

But on this day I laid there thinking about my three children. *How am I going to tell them their dad has Parkinson's?* It would only be a matter of time and my two oldest would be home from college on winter break. My plan was to tell them then. *But how?* It wasn't quite the way I wanted to kick off their holiday break. *But when will there ever be a good time?*

The pounding of the MRI stopped and left me with that residual echo in my head. The gentleman who was performing the MRI (or whatever they do behind the wizard's curtain) slowly pulled me out of the torpedo launcher. There, all smiles, was Christina to greet me—me in my paper smock that exposed my back end like a poorly wrapped Christmas present.

From there Christina escorted me to the anesthesiology department for my spinal tap.

Now, I am only going to describe the details of the spinal tap for those of you who may have one scheduled and want to learn about the procedure, or for those that are just curious.

At the time of this writing we had just celebrated Thanksgiving, so for comparison's sake, imagine having a turkey baster stuck into your back while you're bending over to pull the yams out of the oven—all while someone has battery cables hooked up to your groin.

Ok, I'm exaggerating, a little. We'd never have yams.

Seriously, it wasn't THAT bad. You sit on the side of the bed and prop your feet on a chair in front of you as you lean over a pillow in your lap. Then you hold still—REAL STILL. And you have to keep reminding yourself to breathe. The doctor walks his fingers down your spine until he finds the sweet spot he's looking for. He proceeds to give you a local shot that he (accurately) describes as feeling like a bee sting that will last about ten seconds. And that's exactly what it feels like. Then he pulls out another needle from a sterile package, and although I have never seen it with my own eyes, this is when Christina usually leaves the room. The doctor says, "Ok, Robert, you're going to feel some pressure now," and he's right. It just feels like pressure with a dull ache. Once he's in, it's sit still and wait. Oh, and breathe.

Only once in all the times I have had it done so far (yes, I've had four now), did something out of the ordinary occur. Whether I moved or he moved, all I know is that for a brief moment it felt like someone had hooked up a twelve-volt automotive battery to my groin. An instantaneous shock passed through my... (well, you know) that lit me up and caused one leg to kick out instantaneously.

To which the doctor replied, "Oh! Did I tickle a nerve?"

"Uh huh," I said, taking a deep breath to compose myself. "And I think you brought back my sense of smell!"

CHAPTER 7

COMING CLEAN

The next three-and-a-half months, from November 2012 to the beginning of February 2013 (my next appointment with the Fox Foundation PPMI study), is a period marked by significant changes regarding my relationship with Parkinson's. It's interesting to me as I write this that I used that word. *Relationship.* But with this disease, as I would imagine anyone does with a health issue, you do make your own relationship with it. YOU define what place it will occupy in your life. YOU determine how much space you are going to give it and whether the relationship will be positive or negative.

I was determined from the moment of diagnosis that Parkinson's and I would get along just fine. I was going to make the best of it, always. I was adamant that I did not want others to define me by Parkinson's or, for that matter, let it take over my life in such a way that I allowed Parkinson's to define me. Whatever it decided to take from me, I was set on replacing it with something I had left.

During this time my symptoms became more pronounced to me and began to be noticed by my friends, the latter being one of the first hard doses of reality a new PD patient receives.

Physical challenges started to test my convictions toward maintaining this friendly partnership. I had begun to understand more about the personality of PD, how it has its own unscripted agenda, and that having a "plan" to deal with it is best augmented by learning to be flexible.

To set the tone in my life for this positive relationship, I first had to do some house cleaning. I needed to share this part of my life with my children. I needed to remove the burden that was taking away good energy from me. Then I needed to share my diagnosis with close friends and establish for myself that I was not going to be ashamed of Parkinson's. *It is what it is.* I could choose to be more.

According to the National Parkinson Foundation, Parkinson's is a slowly progressive, neurodegenerative disorder that occurs when certain nerve cells in the brain die or become impaired. Normally these nerve cells produce dopamine, a vital substance that is the chemical messenger responsible for transmitting signals from one relay station of the brain to another, allowing smooth, coordinated function of the body's muscles and movement.

There are **four main motor symptoms** of Parkinson's:

- Shaking or **tremor** (think Muhammad Ali)
- **Slowness** of movement, called bradykinesia (think ME)
- Stiffness or **rigidity** of arms, legs or trunk
- Trouble with balance, or **postural instability**

Along with the main symptoms are a host of secondary **motor** symptoms, including: (The "+" indicates the ones I have experienced.)

- Small, cramped handwriting (+)
- Reduced arm swing on the affected side (+)
- Slight foot drag on the affected side (+)
- "Freezing" or being stuck in place when walking
- Loss of facial expression
- Low vocal volume or hoarse sounding voice (+)
- Tendency to fall backwards
- Walking with a series of quick small steps

The secondary **non-motor** symptoms include:

- Decreased reflexes such as blinking and swallowing (+)
- Dandruff and oily skin

- Constipation
- Sleep disturbances (+)
- Anxiety (+)
- Depression

What was happening to me personally at this time was becoming more and more noticeable in the daily routines of my day. I've often used this analogy when describing it to my friends: You know how when you get a brand new computer and you use it for the first time, you say, "Wow, this is so much faster!" and yet it's probably just nano-seconds we're talking about? Well, I'm the opposite. I used to run so much faster, but now my processor is running slower. For the most part people don't pick up on it, but periodically they do. For me, it's a daily occurrence.

The most noticeable time for me during this particular period was in the shower in the morning. I'd hop in the shower, and with the bar of soap in my right hand would have no problem washing the left side of my body. But once I transferred the bar to my left hand, it was as if my brain didn't know what to do with it. My left hand would move slowly to the right side of my body and then struggle to get going as if the bar were stuck to my skin. The same would happen after putting shampoo in my hands. Once my hands reached my head, it was as if I was trying to pat my head and rub my tummy at the same time. I just couldn't figure out how to do it. I would eventually, but it just took time.

Once out of the shower, it became a struggle to dry off with the towel as efficiently as before.

Buttoning my shirt cuffs became next to impossible, and shaving with a conventional blade became downright dangerous.

I quickly learned to compensate by rolling up my sleeves when I could, or wearing pullovers or t-shirts.

A day in my office was becoming an increasingly struggle due to my cramped handwriting, hand fatigue using the keyboard, and general exhaustion I'd feel by day's end due to my poor sleep at night. I was also starting to get concerned about presentations due to my lack of focus, still feeling "ungrounded" and my voice that, by the end of the day, would be going hoarse.

My solution: Plan important meetings and presentations for the mornings.

Every day became an evaluation of my symptoms and I was finding it difficult to forget about my newly found friend; my hopes for a wonderful relationship were getting off to a rocky start. Luckily, for all outward appearances I was doing a good job and as far as I knew no one was noticing. *I can do this.*

I am blessed with some of the most fantastic friendships a person could ask for: people from college, work, neighbors and high school. Some of my high school friends are the most special of all. For most people high school friendships don't last or, at the very least, don't continue as they did in high school. But in my case they have and they've become even richer.

I grew up in a town called Downers Grove, Illinois, a town recently named in a poll as one of the ten friendliest towns in the United States. Not surprising to me! I went to Downers Grove North High School—the Trojans—and graduated in a class of well over eight hundred students.

So here it is, some thirty-plus years after our graduation, and a large group of us continue to get together at any opportunity. It was at one of those occasions at a pub back in our hometown that I realized, for the first time, that my symptoms are not something I am always keenly aware of, nor are they always hidden from view.

As about twenty or thirty friends filled one room of the bar, a large number of us had pushed together a group of tables so we could chat and reminisce. I was sitting at one end of the table drinking a vodka and cranberry (my Russian neurologist fully approves), when one of my friends at the far end of the table calls out to the others who flanked me on both sides, "You better cut Bob off! I think he might have had too much."

To which I queried back, "What makes you say that?" thinking maybe I had been slurring my words.

But what transpired next was my first opportunity to see myself through the eyes of another—I sat there and was able to watch myself. She picked up her glass and brought it, ever so slowly, up to her mouth, noting how unhurriedly I had just been doing the same. I hadn't been aware of it at all.

Now approximately a month later after she learned of my diagnosis from a friend, she expressed to me that she felt terrible about what transpired that evening, and I have told her repeatedly that it did not bother me in the least—and I mean that. Her intentions were good. She was actually speaking from her heart and was concerned about my well-being, thinking I'd had too much to drink. In all actuality, I owe her a debt of thanks, as it was instrumental in getting me to make changes that had positive results.

Again, we never know where the messages we need may come from.

CHAPTER 8

A NEED FOR A CHANGE

The clothes were starting to be left wherever they were taken off, towels were on the bathroom floor, lights were left on, dishes were piling up in the kitchen sink, and half-empty Coke Zero cans were strewn throughout the house.

It wasn't that my Parkinson's was making my daily activities and tasks more difficult to accomplish.

My girls were home from college.

I honestly don't know where the pig gene showed up in my bloodline but my girls have issues with neatness. They definitely have problems picking up their clothes. If you've ever had the pleasure of seeing the movie *Edward Scissorhands* with Johnny Depp, you'll recall there is a scene where he's creating an ice sculpture and the chips of ice are flying about as he shapes and carves with his razor sharp appendages. That's the way it looks when my girls go into their drawers to pick out clothes. The hands dive in, arms flail about and the clothes start to fly and rain down on the room.

Maybe it was payback for the things I did while raising them.

Having had daughters first, I, like most fathers, thought about the prospect of my daughters eventually dating, which scared me to death because I clearly remember my interest in girls as an adolescent teenager. My son was not a concern. I know, a double standard, but that's a father's right.

So I decided very early on not to potty train my daughters. Think about it—it's brilliant. The boy comes to the house to pick up my daughter and take her out on a date. He does his best imitation of Eddie Haskell from *Leave It To Beaver*, complimenting my wife… "Gee, you're looking lovely today Mrs. B.," while flashing his smile and giving thumbs-up to me. Then he tells me how he'll have her home nice and early, all the while my knowing very well that the intentions of this sixteen-year-old, five foot four runt, packed with raging hormones, is about to suck the lips off my daughter's face. But…surprise! You *will* have her home early, because when you take her to the movies and feed her popcorn, candy and soda, she's going to have an accident and you're going to *have* to bring her home.

Well, it didn't quite ever happen that way because my wife stepped in and we eventually raised them *her* way. But a father can dream. Suffice it to say, I did have my moments of embarrassing them.

Nevertheless, regardless of how our relationship had been fashioned to date, now was the time I needed to sit down with my kids and tell them my news.

It was one evening a week before Christmas. The kids were each in their rooms on iPads, computers, or phones. I swear I don't know how my generation survived our youth not having the technology that they have nowadays. My wife and I were in our bedroom watching TV and I felt that now was the right time. I turned off the TV and opening the door to our room called out into the hall, would they all please come into our room. By the time they were filing in, I had taken a seat on the floor. Each came in and sat down and one of them said, "What's up?" The concern on my face must have been clear, because the expression on each of theirs quickly became serious. The focus and attention they gave me was amazingly foreign to me. *Maybe I should lead with a conversation about cleaning their rooms? No, maybe not.*

"There's something I've been meaning to share with you for some time now, but there just hasn't been a good time to tell you. This past July I was diagnosed with Parkinson's. And I want you to know that I am doing fine with it."

There was silence.

I went on to say, "There are a lot of people that are living with Parkinson's and continue to have productive lives. Michael J. Fox has lived with it for well over twenty years and Muhammad Ali, close to thirty."

I reassured them, "You do not die from Parkinson's disease."

"I'm really ok with this and I want you to know that," I said. "The only thing that worries or concerns me is how you will see me. I don't ever want to be a burden to you and have you resent me for having this."

Then the tears started to come to my eyes. And the tears started to come to theirs.

It's hard for a child to see their parent vulnerable. It's hard to see someone you look to for strength appear weak. I understood that and felt bad that they had to see me that way. But I wanted to show them that it's always ok to be open and honest about your feelings.

It's hard for a parent, too, to see your child taking on this hurt, worry and concern on your behalf. It's part of that burden I didn't want to give them. But as if there were magnets in each of our hearts, they all, simultaneously, came over and hugged me.

We cried for a while together until my oldest daughter was able to alter the mood of the moment.

She pulled away from me briefly and wiping away the tears from her face, looked at me with a serious expression and said, "You've always told us how few diapers you changed when we were little, Dad..."

"Yes," I said, wondering what this had to do with my announcement.

"I just want you to know: I won't be changing yours."

We all had a good laugh and everything returned to a more constructive dialogue. I informed my kids that at this point that I did not want them to say anything to the rest of the family because I wasn't ready yet, but that I would when the time was right.

I had already made the decision to not tell my only brother, his wife and my two nieces. They were busy dealing with health dilemmas within their own family and I didn't want to distract their focus with my own issues. I figured once things had settled down for them, there would be plenty of time.

But what would become one of my greatest internal struggles with my feelings was my conviction that I was not going to tell my parents. Ever.

My mom is seventy-six and my dad, eighty-four. I just couldn't rationalize in my head how telling them did them any good or did myself any good either. There was nothing they could do for me. I would merely be giving them a burden to carry for the remainder of their years that, in my mind, could ultimately do more harm than good to their already fragile health.

I explained my rationale to my kids, but I have to be honest and say that what I saw and felt in my heart with clarity and conviction was met with far less support than I had hoped for. My son in particular was very adamant that I was completely wrong, that my parents had every right to know and how would I feel if something was wrong with one of my children and they chose not to tell me? I argued that it was not the same and that they were missing the point. There was nothing positive for my parents to gain, and that I was worried about them at this stage of their lives.

I had made my decision, I was making it from my heart and I was asking them to respect it.

Everyone agreed to disagree. They would respect my wishes, but not support my decision.

That's ok, I thought to myself. *After all, attitudes can change over time.*

CHAPTER 9

GEORGE CARLIN, HEAVEN & HELL AND THE BEATLES

My third appointment with the Michael J. Fox Foundation PPMI study in February of 2013 was highly uneventful. We reviewed all of my symptoms (which I've outlined here to this point) and they still were relatively unchanged. Blood was drawn and urine was analyzed. I was questioned about my mood and sanity. Repeats of the cognitive tests were done, like the word associations, memory tests and the tap-along-to-letters test, all to gauge my level of change and progress. I was still cruising along and doing very well.

My next appointment was scheduled for the three months later, the beginning of May. Apparently, Parkinson's disease progresses on a quarterly basis.

Which makes this a good time to share the foundation of my spirituality and beliefs. As I continue writing, there will be events that I'll start to share that begin to "shake up" my realm of comfort, reawakening my thirst for knowledge and my understanding of life. I begin to personally draw on those beliefs to gather strength for managing and living with my Parkinson's.

Before going into depth about my spirituality, I feel it prudent to restate an excerpt from the Preface:

"...The thoughts I share regarding my spirituality are not intended to pass judgment on anyone's religion, faith, or belief, or to promote my views. They are

simply my thoughts and ideas regarding my spirituality, and an observation of how my spiritual growth is being affected by Parkinson's (and vice versa).

This book is an opportunity for me to share my experience with other Parkinson's patients, both newly diagnosed as well as seasoned professionals. It is also a chance for me to work through my thoughts about both my faith and Parkinson's by writing them down. Most of all, I hope that it paints a meaningful representation for my children of who their father is and what he is about."

Okay. So if at any time while reading this, you find yourself feeling angry, threatened, or the need to evangelize me as a result of what I might express here, please come back here and read this excerpt again, because what you are feeling was not my intent.

~Thank you.

The comedian George Carlin once said, and I paraphrase here: "Religion is like a pair of shoes. For some people it helps them walk a straighter path. And for others it only hurts their feet. I don't think it is our responsibility to fit people with shoes they do not want to wear."

When I first heard that expressed, I thought his words were brilliant. Comedians have a rare gift for conveying the truth in humorous ways. We laugh or smile at first, but when we're left to ponder the message, we often are enlightened.

For me, what George Carlin said very accurately summed up my feelings. He clearly and succinctly expresses the importance and VALUE of religion in a great number of people's lives, that religion, indeed, *does* help individuals live and walk a straighter path. He in no way denies the importance that religion plays in guiding *certain* people toward a path of living a life of love, kindness and respect for all living creatures. But what he also expresses, is that organized religion is not *required* by all human beings to achieve an awareness to feel that love, respect and kindness for all living things or to live a good life. For some people, that desire to "love thy neighbor as thyself" is already in the root of their soul.

The key to me in George Carlin's statement is CHOICE. Everyone has the right to worship in whatever way best nourishes his or her soul. At the same time, we all should have respect for the choices of others.

My belief is that *how* an individual ultimately reaches the goal of being able to love everyone, care for all, have respect for everyone's thoughts and ideas, and come to the realization that *we all* are connected to each other, does not matter. The final result is what we each need individually.

The Beatles had that down: "All you need is love."

Now a religion, or better yet, a person that has no tolerance for another's religion, and kills in the name of their God, I have no respect for. Likewise, fitting other people with shoes they do not want is not showing tolerance, acceptance or love for who they are, the way they are, and how they choose to believe.

I choose to look at the person. I choose to try to see their heart. If they are Buddhist, Muslim, Catholic, Protestant, Jewish, atheist, whatever, that does not matter to me, as long as their actions, thoughts and deeds are not to hurt others, but are centered in love and respect. Good people and good souls come from every religion and every walk of life.

I do not consider myself religious. I *do* consider myself very spiritual. I do not condemn *any* religion, and I also do not go out of my way to promote spirituality. I believe in choice and tolerance.

But to explain my path...

I was raised in the Christian faith and attended a Methodist church from the time of my baptism through confirmation, into my teenage years. I attended Sunday school regularly, sang in the choir and attended youth retreats and the like. My religious experience, for me personally, presented the opportunity for introspection, to look at my life in the context of a much bigger picture. But I was an adolescent who never ceased to ask questions. I was also in tune, from a very early age, with my intuition, from my heart, my mind and my gut.

There were things that I questioned about my own religion because they didn't sit true in my heart. "Why do I have to pay the church in order for God to hear my prayers?" I'd ask my mom. "And why do I have to go to the church to have God hear me? Doesn't God hear me when I'm not in his house?" The logic just didn't make sense.

My mom is a woman of deep-rooted faith and is extremely devoted to her church, her beliefs and her faith in God, so my questioning of that faith was met with her grave concern that she had somehow failed me as a Christian mother. I know she probably still holds that concern to this day. I did my best, however, to reassure her that she had not failed, that I felt good in my heart about who I was, but that I simply had questions.

If my church espouses to be the "correct" religion, that its teachings are the gospel of God, and that through them I will find eternal salvation, then what about all these other religions? Are all of their followers wrong and are all of those children of God doomed? Is my all-loving God capable of denying this bounty of other souls? Because they were born into a family that chose one religion over another, either by demographics or mere happenstance, are they all to be denied a place in heaven? I just couldn't fathom it.

At one point of desperation, I recall my mother saying to me, "Robert, can I ask you if you believe in Jesus Christ?"

"Absolutely!" I said to my mother.

"I believe in Jesus Christ. I also believe in the Dali Lama, Martin Luther King, Jr., Mother Teresa, Gandhi, John Lennon, Abraham, Buddha, and a host of other individuals that have lived on this earth, who all got the big picture. They each felt in their heart and soul the true message of love, respect, forgiveness and caring for fellow human beings. They all understood the great connection we all share. They knew that there is a greater energy that ties us all together."

And if I were saying this to my mom today, I would add Nelson Mandela to that list.

These leaders came from different countries, religions and circumstances in life, but to me they all carried a universal message. It was clear to me that at the root of all religions was one common theme: love.

Love would become my foundation for the belief system I would carry with me as I journeyed forward, being always mindful of a greater connection, and that the energy all around me is not separate from me, but a part of me. I believe that the people I come in contact with in my daily life—my friends, my family and those I meet by chance—are all part of a connected world. If I *try* to make my decisions from my heart and from a place of love, I cannot go wrong.

I emphasized the word *try* because it's all been a life of experience—not good or bad, just experiences. Some events that others view as bad, I view as learning experiences—ones I choose not to repeat, but a step toward spiritual growth, nonetheless. I've made plenty of mistakes, but quite a few of those events have changed the direction of my life for the better.

When I felt as though I was drowning, someone lent me a hand. When I was going one direction in life, something spun me around to point me in a new direction. And when a man needed a bone marrow transplant, a five-year-old girl gave up her life.

My mom would say that's God at work and, though not in her way, I would agree, because my God—or essence, or energy, or Creator—is the sum of all of us. We each are a small piece of this one big energy, and it is the sum of us and all things that are living that bring about the reality of God. We keep looking elsewhere for wherever God is, and we neglect to look at ourselves. When children are starving we ask how God can let this happen when indeed, *we* are the energy for change. It is all of us—our love and spirit at work in the energy of connections, friendships, and chance interactions—that changes direction in each other's lives every day.

My theory for myself (and my apologies to John Lennon): Imagine for a moment that each of us represents a small piece of God or a portion of this bigger energy in the universe. As such, we all have the powers of God to create life and effect change. Through those "God-given" talents, our individual purpose, here in this life, is to educate and elevate our own souls towards a greater God-like quality through the deeds we do and the way we treat others.

Now imagine that, at the end of this life, you were given the opportunity to judge yourself and the life you just led. There's no separate entity judging you—after all, you are a piece of God—and at this time you will be completely impartial. You will either conclude you have lived your life to the very best of your ability and that your soul has learned everything it requires to reside in "heaven" (the ultimate connection with other like souls, together which the sum of is God or the utmost energy). Or you choose to repeat this "hell" and do it all over again, in the hope that the next time, you'll do a little better.

Additionally, throw in the idea that perhaps we are not alone, that there are other pieces of God/knowledge/energy at play on our behalf. Through our positive thoughts (prayers?), we draw guidance and direction into our own lives.

Give yourself the opportunity to live your life mindful that others are equally important, both in their own individual journeys and in yours as well. Any person who may come into your life has the potential to be a profound gift. Likewise, you may hold this gift for others.

From this theory comes my personal belief of "new souls" and "old souls" those early in their journey as compared to others who have lived lives repeatedly and "get it."

I see others finding their energy and path through their own religion and their own heart and I am happy for them. How they get to where they are ultimately going is not my personal concern.

For me, I choose to see my friendships, my connections and the chance encounters I have as gifts, messengers and traffic cops in the journey of my life. I am grateful for all they have brought to me and how they have helped me on my way.

I choose to see my Parkinson's not as a hardship, but rather an experience to make the best of. Maybe it holds a gift I can share with others or it is a gift that was given to me that will profoundly change the direction of my life. That remains to be seen.

There is one thing I have learned very recently though, and that is that I have long been one who seeks to know the answers too quickly. As a result of that focus, I have often missed the knowledge that comes from the journey of discovery. *Tremors* is retracing the steps of that journey and I've promised myself that I'll enjoy the walk from here on out.

Parkinson's is definitely "shaking up" my world.

CHAPTER 10

BEND AND STRETCH

"You know you're getting old when sleeping in the wet spot means you've just rolled over onto the drool on your pillow."

Getting old, or dealing with Parkinson's.

It turns out that an increase in saliva in the mouth due to less frequent swallowing is also common amongst Parkinson's patients.

"Really?"

It's just another strange symptom, along with decreased blinking and losing your sense of smell. I'm batting three for three, so it's no wonder I've chosen to keep a sense of humor about Parkinson's. (I actually wrote that joke myself, thank you very much.)

As I began to open up and share the news of my diagnosis, I had a pretty standard opening with everyone I told: "Hey, I'm looking on the bright side… if worse comes to worse I can always get a job with Home Depot as a paint can shaker or a local bar as a martini shaker." That usually drew a laugh and I soon realized it put people at ease. The humor removed a little fear for them and allowed for a constructive dialogue to take place.

As much as I joke—I believe keeping a sense of humor is tremendously therapeutic—when it comes to Parkinson's, laughter is not the best medicine.

Exercise is.

Just three years prior, at the age of fifty, I was in the best shape of my life: toned, fit and with energy to burn. But by my fifty-third birthday I had managed to let all of my good habits quickly slip away. That which took years to accomplish, I washed away in as little as six months.

As my Parkinson's symptoms slowly became more pronounced and the exhaustion of working through a day set in, I became complacent. I would come home from work, have dinner with my wife and son and go sit down in a chair in our bedroom until I was ready to turn in. I was spent. Exhausted. Both physically and mentally.

I had given up my membership at the gym where I had been working out, rationalizing that it was not worth the expense, especially when the economy was struggling. And I certainly felt I could no longer put myself through the paces that a gym of that nature required.

I was looking for excuses.

Some time ago, Dr. Simuni had provided me with a booklet on exercise as well as a few things that Parkinson's patients could do to help maintain a better quality of life. However, after perusing the pages and seeing men and women in their eighties and nineties sitting in chairs working with rubber bands, I determined, *That's not me!* and quickly tossed them aside. I didn't heed the advice. Little did I realize that if I did not change my ways, that that would be me at sixty.

What transpired next was once again proof of how individuals in my life have repeatedly played an important role in altering my path.

A dear friend told me the story of her father who'd had Parkinson's and likewise had not put in the effort to keep moving. She knew firsthand the importance, and the consequences, of not pushing yourself physically when it was easiest to just quit. She shared with me the pain she felt watching what this disease did to her father, and stressed that it was important I take the opportunity to keep fit while I had it, so that my children wouldn't have to go through the same.

Dr. Simuni as well went a little farther to say that she was not recommending exercise to me as a choice—she was prescribing exercise for me as my doctor. I was reminded of our earlier discussions when I had asked if she would step up for me when I could benefit from something outside of the study.

That February I bought a birthday gift for myself: fitness, in the form of a treadmill and an exercise bike. I combined it with a weight bench I had at my office, and set up a small gym in my home.

The treadmill has become my metaphor for another new path toward managing my Parkinson's. I wake up every day at 5 a.m. and head downstairs in the dark to hop on the treadmill. I walk, on average, for an hour at a time. I use that time to meditate. I use that time to energize. And I use that time to give thanks for all I have. The results have been remarkable. My energy is back up, as is my strength and my focus. I don't miss a day.

The literature Dr. Simuni gave me also outlined additional ways patients can supplement their individual exercise programs, including yoga, tai chi and massage therapy.

I had long been a proponent of massage. Being a business owner, I had received a massage regularly every month for a good fifteen years for relaxation and stress relief. until my massage therapist married and moved away I had looked for some time to replace her, but never had success finding someone with her intuition. She just had a way of finding knots and stress in my body that I didn't even know I had.

Now that I was feeling reinvigorated, I put the positive thought out to the universe and started my search again. Little did I know at the time the remarkable person I would find along this path. I would find a spiritual teacher. A shaman. A healer. A guide.

The new exercise program for my body was about to start exercising my mind and my spirit.

CHAPTER 11

12:34

Throughout my writing, I have continually made reference to the messages, connections and communications I believe we all have at play within our lives, and the significance I place on them for myself. I've recounted a few personal instances in which I felt my path in life, as well as the paths of others, were changed as a result of being receptive to those events, cues and signs.

How these messages are delivered to us, as well as how they are received (or maybe better said, perceived), vary widely in their form. It can be a direct sign that we see with our eyes, such as the blood drive flyer in the grocery store for the little five-year-old girl with leukemia, that ultimately leads to a bone marrow donation for a man half way around the world; or perhaps the sparkle of sunlight on a car's side mirror that alerts a driver to that oncoming car.

I've also received messages through dreams so vivid that they were difficult to distinguish from reality.

And then there are just strange things like repeatedly seeing a digital clock, be it in my home, on my car radio or on my computer, at precisely 12:34. Is it some sort of message or just my whimsical mind?

A common method we all use to receive information comes through our senses of touch, sight, sound and smell. But what I tend to find for myself, personally, is that I am most receptive to the messages and energies around me through my intuition. A lot of people believe, as do I, that your intuition is the essence of your soul. It is where your true knowledge and understanding of *yourself* resides. It is your heart, your mind and your gut.

I used to see these cues with just my eyes, but as I became open to feeling something more, a communication took place at a much deeper level. I learned that empathy can be another tool for your intuition.

I've often said to my children when they're faced with a tough decision, "Listen to your heart. If you do what feels right in your heart, in your soul, then you can't go wrong. It may not turn out as you hoped, but if the decision was made from your heart, then you'll have remained true to *yourself*."

A much more profound form of intuitive communication happened to me in my late twenties, when I received a very clear and strong premonition.

One of my first jobs out of college was as a graphic designer for a computer software publisher called Mindscape, in a suburb of Chicago. A group of coworkers and I had made a trek to Milwaukee at the end of one summer week for a Friday evening out on the town. The interesting thing about Milwaukee on a weekend night, at least in the late eighties, was the streets always seemed to be deserted. There was always ample parking downtown and it was always an easy city to walk from one establishment to another.

As our evening wrapped up, a group of nine or ten of us began walking back to our cars along one of these desolate streets. The night was clear and the sidewalks were well lit with street lamps overhead. As we walked along, laughing and chatting, we pretty much took up the width of the entire sidewalk. My position in relation to the rest of the group was such that I was walking "shotgun", at the front and on the street side.

About three blocks ahead of us along our route, was a man who was leaning against a parking sign next to the curb. His back was completely to us, so I could not see his face.

Almost as quickly as I gained sight of him a conversation began to occur in my head that I felt in my gut. *There's something wrong here—this doesn't feel right,* a voice in my head whispered. My eyes became locked on this motionless figure.

The conversation amongst my friends continued as if no one else had this same sense of concern. I found myself giving half-heartfelt laughs in the verbal exchange as we continued to walk.

Two more blocks.

My position in the group and the path we were taking was going to bring me right along the left side of this man. It was like driving down a highway and seeing a car on the shoulder of the road ahead but you have semi trucks beside you that make changing lanes impossible. You just grip the steering wheel, keep your eye on the car and hold your course.

However, in this case, the further I continued down this path, the more real the sense of danger became, as if the car on the side of the road was suddenly going to open its door.

Now there are some who believe, as I do, in the Law of Attraction. It's the idea behind the book and movie, *The Secret* by Rhonda Byrne, which says, a person's thoughts put out into the universe bring back to them the equivalent. Everything is vibrational: your thoughts, your ideas, every being. You will draw to yourself whatever vibration matches yours, wanted or unwanted. Think positive thoughts and positive results will dominate your life. Conversely, think negative thoughts and you most likely receive a lot of disappointment and failure. Like attracts like.

One might think that what was happening along this downtown Milwaukee street, was that I was putting out the thought/vibration that something bad was going to happen; therefore the matching vibration/result was destined to come back to me.

To me, it's a debate of which occurred first. Was it my intuition receiving an outside message? Or was I consciously putting out a thought that was going to bring about the event? I do not have the answer to that. As far as I am concerned, I am in my infancy in regards to learning about and understanding the events that have occurred in my life in relation to my own spirituality and beliefs. That is why I am writing. I am chronicling the events in my life that have taken place to date, the new occurrences as they happen, and the steps I continually undertake to learn about and grow my own spirituality in order to ultimately discover how they effect, and are affected by, my Parkinson's.

Learning how to better receive, read, interpret, understand and send out positive messages in my universe is all a part of this process as well.

All I do know is that at this time, in Milwaukee, I am about to get hit. It's kind of ironic because a premonition or intuitive event like this is sometimes referred to as a "hit" when you receive information this way.

Three more short strides will bring me right next to this man who has never turned around the entire time. I'm no longer talking to any of my friends and, in all honesty, I couldn't have told you if any conversation was even taking place. In my head there wasn't a sound other than my heartbeat and my thoughts. I'm watching intently with all senses heightened.

In the blink of an eye, his left arm, which had been down at his side, snaps upward with military precision, bending at the elbow while making a fist. The back of his closed left hand is swinging with ever-increasing speed, with the obvious intent of landing squarely in my face.

Because of my intense awareness of the moment, my hand moved simultaneously, catching his fist with a grip that stopped just inches from my face.

Everyone in our group stopped in disbelief and watched as the man turned around, his fist still gripped by mine, looked me directly in the eye and said, "You're talking too loud." To which I apologized, slowly released his hand and walked away.

To this day, I question whether his reference was directed toward our group and the conversation we had been having as we walked, or whether he was talking directly to me and referring to the thoughts I was sending out to the universe. If it was the latter, my apologies to the universe. From now on, I'll try to keep it down.

CHAPTER 12

A HARD PILL TO SWALLOW

When it comes to prescription medicine, it's always been a love/hate relationship for me. I think a big part of that is simply due to my own ignorance on what's really behind the chemistry. I mean, I'm a "sensitive artist type", not a Bunsen-burner-and-beaker kind of guy. When I could have been concentrating my efforts in science class, I took a greater interest in coloring outside the lines. As a result, I'm chemically challenged and run a design business. Combine that with a skeptical and questioning nature, and it is no wonder that making the decision to start prescription medications for my Parkinson's disease was a difficult one for me.

I will say I fully appreciate the benefits of some prescription drugs, especially as they relate to pain management.

From the age of twenty-three until the time I'm writing this, I have given birth approximately twenty-five times to some of the cutest, most adorable kidney stones. I am a chronic stone producer. I make kidney stones so regularly that I should get a rock polisher and go into the jewelry business: Bob's Bladder Baubles. I have passed a good ninety-five percent of them and have had surgery twice. I do know pain and I do know the power of medicine for pain management. When you have a kidney stone, narcotics can be your best friend.

With the benefits of medications, also come risks. Obviously, narcotics should not be abused, as they are extremely addictive and dangerous if not taken properly. But even milder, over-the-counter products can be risky if not taken on the advice of a doctor. There is one nasal spray I use that is amazing— I swear it could open up our shower drain and power through all the hair from three women in our house. It definitely can help you breathe. But after a week or so of continuous use, the "rebound effect" kicks in and you're hooked. What once provided twelve hours of relief is now down to two minutes and you're using that bottle like you're a mayor from Canada.

And Chapstick! What is in that stuff? My wife swears by Chapstick and uses it all the time. She says her lips feel great because of it, and if she doesn't use it then her lips will get really dry and crack. Crack is right. It's addictive. Chapstick is crack for your lips.

Seriously, I sometimes wonder if prescription medications can bring about those same dependencies and exacerbate the very symptoms they are intended to treat. To say the least, I have questions and I am skeptical.

Prior to my next appointment in May of 2013 with the Michael J. Fox Foundation PPMI study, I was increasingly taking note of (and being given notice of) a change in my symptoms. The first situation was earlier in the year when I was out with high school friends at a bar and a good friend mimicked my slow drinking motion, thinking I had had too much to drink. The second time was when our family went out for barbecued ribs. After everyone had finished their dinner, I realized I had only cut and eaten three ribs. And finally, my day-to-day tasks of showering, dressing and working at the computer were becoming less efficient.

When I met with Dr. Simuni and she inquired as to how I was doing, I did not hesitate to bring her up to date. After completing the necessary evaluations and tests scheduled for the day, Dr. Simuni returned to the subject of my physical slowness. She proceeded to explain to me that there were medications available that she could start me on, if I felt I was ready.

She must have sensed my hesitancy in the expression on my face, because without my having said a word, she went on and asked, "What are you afraid of, Robert?"

"Oh, I'm not afraid of any of it, Dr. Simuni," I said. "I simply am enjoying very much being a part of the study here and I want to remain a part of it."

Dr. Simuni replied, "You've met the six-month threshold we hope for patients to achieve, Robert. We have established your baseline of data while not on medications. Regardless of whether or not you start medications, you are, and will remain, a part of this study for five years—or as long as you want to continue to participate. If you choose to start medications, we can take that into account in our research and findings."

She looked at me and smiled as if to say, "Is there something else?"

Again, I'm sure she saw my hesitancy, but this time I spoke up and said, "Well, I'm also concerned that by starting a medication, that I might somehow be creating a need for more and more medication down the road and that I might be bringing on new symptoms sooner—like I'm accelerating the process."

I paused briefly and then said, "And I also keep thinking that, comparatively to many other Parkinson's patients, my symptoms probably don't appear too severe and they do not keep me from doing anything. I just do them slowly."

The answer Dr. Simuni gave to me is why I like and respect her so much. Her comments are always honest, candid and direct.

"Robert, I must reiterate to you that all we are doing is treating the symptoms. There is no clinical evidence that would support the idea that the medicines would create a reliance on them or make your condition worse. However, Parkinson's is a progressive disease. That is a fact. How it will progress for you or for the next person, we do not know. And if, at any time, you decide you want to stop taking a medicine, you are free to stop."

I knew I had one more reason for hesitation on my part, but I kept that thought to myself. Giving Dr. Simuni a smile, I said, "Let's give it a try then. I would like to start some treatment and see how it goes."

"Ok, then," she said as she stood up and shook my hand. "I will get Melanie and have her tell you about the medicine you will be starting on."

"Thank you, Dr. Simuni," I said as she left.

As I sat there briefly alone with my thoughts, I realized: I had taken the next step.

~

Neupro 8MG Extended Release. Worn as a patch on the skin for 24hrs/day. Acts as a dopamine agonist (activates the dopamine receptors in the brain in the absence of dopamine).

Azilect 2MG tablet. Once/day. (Dr. Simuni has done research showing potential of Azilect to slow the progression of Parkinson's disease. Clinical data is yet to be conclusive.)

Exercise Treadmill/Core/Weights. 1 hr. walk (600 cal), 20 min ab work, 20 min weight work.

CHAPTER 13

PERSPECTIVE

I've been of the belief that, how we see and interpret our world determines how we react and respond to the events in our life. The way we choose to manage our thoughts ultimately defines our reality. There really are no rules on how you have to see things. The choice of interpretation and the perception of the experience are completely individual.

The simplest example is in the observation that one person sees the glass as half empty while the other sees the glass as half full. It's the same glass and the same amount of liquid, and I would venture to guess that the signals to the optic nerves are, for all intents and purposes, the same; yet, the interpretations are entirely different.

Do the experiences we have (and have had) in our lives shape our outlook? Or does the outlook that we hold determine the experiences that we will have? I think it's a bit of both.

Perception, outlook and expectations are definitely something I am thinking about more and more in regards to my Parkinson's. I believe very strongly that I can change the course of this disease simply by the way I choose to look at the experience.

Likewise, the experiences I have had—and continue to have—in my life, are reinforcing my spirituality as I continue my journey.

I'm definitely not new to bringing a different perspective to things. As a child, I felt an early connection to my universe and I always had a unique way of looking at things. "Askew" is probably the best word to describe it.

Perhaps that was a precursor of things to come and showed my creative, artistic side at an early age. I just recall being easily engaged by the images and thoughts about my world that I could conjure up in my mind.

If it were summertime—one of those days that lasted forever, when the sky was perfectly clear, painted a rich, robin's egg blue—it would not have been uncommon for my mother to look out the window and see me lying on the ground in our backyard, staring up at the sky. I'd lay there like a snow angel, arms and legs stretched as wide as possible to each side, with each hand clenching onto a clump of grass. As I lay there staring up into the blue abyss, I'd actually rotate my perspective 180 degrees in my mind, and imagine that I was no longer looking up into the sky, but rather that I was holding on to Mother Earth, or hanging on the surface of this planet to keep from free falling downward into that perfectly blue ocean below. The occasional bird that flew by was the silhouette of a fish beneath the water's surface. A cloud was the white cap of a wave. And if I stared long enough, I could imagine a boat sailing by as well.

I allowed myself to see my world differently, and in doing so I created a greater sense of connection with my world. I wasn't just standing or lying on the earth, being held there by gravity. In my mind I had a relationship or partnership with the planet for survival. In that moment, not only was I holding onto her, but she onto me.

I've had other experiences over time where, learning to look at and feel things differently, took something that was once very frightening and turned it into something I found comfort in.

As a child, the vivid imagination that entertained me by day, relentlessly tormented me by night with a recurrent nightmare that would leave me screaming for my parents.

The irony was that it all had to do with perspective. In my dream, I was in a vast room void of all furniture, carpet and draperies. There were no people in the room, nor doors or windows, no light fixtures overhead. It was lonely and it was solitary. It was void of everything. Like a big, blank canvas, the walls, ceiling and floor appeared to be varying hues of gray.

My vantage point in the room was from a seated position on the floor, facing toward one corner of the room. I could see in front of me the three distinct lines or axis of the room: Straight ahead, the vertical line where wall met wall; to my right, a horizontal line where the wall met the floor, meeting the centerline in front of me; and to my left was its horizontal sister line, traversing the other side of the room and meeting the other two. All three intersected in the very corner of the room, and there my eyes were fixed.

Ever so slowly, my body was drawn in closer and closer to that corner. I could feel myself being forced further downward, tighter and tighter into that corner with the three surfaces surrounding me. There was that ever-present feeling of no escape. Just when I would think it was impossible to go any further, I would awaken to the crash of my body as I fell out of bed, landing hard on the floor, my sheets twisted tight around me like a toga wrap gone badly, my forehead dripping in sweat and my heart racing fast.

In all honesty, the screams that shattered the night were not screams of terror from my dream, but from the waking imagination of a young boy. As I sat startled awake there in the middle of my bedroom floor, my eyes would dart about the room imagining the assortment of boogiemen that lurked under my bed and in dark corners, as well as the kind of vermin that only took off after the movement of little boys in the dark. So best to just sit still and scream at the top of my lungs until my parents come in and turned on the lights.

The curious thing that has happened over time, though, is that the same visualization that was the core of the nightmare has now become an effective form of "counting sheep". I can now lay down to bed at night and take that visual journey through the lines of my blank room and find a method of relaxation that sends me peacefully off to sleep. A change of outlook was all that was needed.

I'm convinced that with my Parkinson's, I'll eliminate the boogiemen, too.

CHAPTER 14

A MOUTHFUL

Growing up in a home with just one brother left me with the distinct impression that, if we had just had a sister in the house, there most definitely would have been more peace. After all, girls were all frilly and played with dolls and giggled. They would have just naturally diluted the testosterone that was rampant in my house.

That viewpoint changed quickly when I had two daughters of my own.

With girls, there are moods and emotions as varied as the shades of their nail polish. When they fight, well, you might as well just work late at the office. Not that I ever did that. I was sincerely busy and had to work late.

With a brother, however, it was clear which emotion was at play from one hour to the next. You knew exactly how each of us felt at the moment. There were only two possibilities: we were either hugging and laughing or punching and crying—not too much gray area in between. Being the younger and considerably smaller brother, I was usually on the losing end of the fights. Growing up, there were only two times that I can recall when the decision in the bout went to me—and they both came at a point where I snapped.

The first was around the age of three or four, when my fighting skills were at their least developed. I had reached a point where I had taken all the shoves and hits a wobbly toddler could. After a confrontation with my brother, as he stood naked at his dresser getting a change of clothes out of one of the drawers, I ran up behind him and, like an attacking Doberman

Pinscher, sunk my tiny teeth into one of the cheeks of his butt.—I mean *sunk them in*. Had I gone a little bit further or had a little more pent-up anger, I might have taken a chunk out like Mike Tyson.

The second time was about eight years later when my brother was sixteen and I was twelve. Like many teenagers, my brother was saddled with a mouthful of braces. This was during a time when there wasn't such a thing as invisible braces—no, these were all bright and shiny. To me, the metal looked like razor wire on a prison fence and I guess in a way they were holding his teeth captive.

Once again, I had reached a breaking point in a fight with my brother when I felt I had been pushed into a corner. I was again outmatched by size and strength. When a fighter is put in the corner and it seems the match is going to be lost, the best thing to do is just cover up, conserve some energy and gather some strength to make one concentrated effort to fight your way out.

I came out swinging and landed one solidly on my brother's mouth. The impact of the punch imbed flesh into metal, but ultimately left the impression not only on my fist, but my heart. I didn't like hurting anyone—especially my brother.

Now my brother and I are in our fifties and at this particular time in our lives there is quite a bit of gray area between us, in part, because my brother wasn't aware of my diagnosis. I was again in the corner, covering up.

Two years earlier when the stress with work, economy and my health were all just taking shape, I had vaguely mentioned to my brother how I had been feeling a bit "off." I'd been dealing with problems at the office, having some anxiety, not feeling like myself, that sort of thing. The truth of it was, I was in the midst of trying to figure things out and I really didn't have any concrete answers to share with him. Well, either he never forgot about that, or once my Parkinson's diagnosis had been privately confirmed to me, my symptoms were now apparent to him as well. It seemed that on every occasion that brought the family together, be it a birthday or holiday, inevitably there would be a moment where it was just he and I, and he'd inquisitively ask, "So, how are you feeling?"

I would reply in a non-committal way, "I'm OK." If pushed any further, I'd say, "It's really nothing to talk about right now."

The problem, however, as I had mentioned earlier, was that my diagnosis coincided with some family health issues my brother's family was dealing with. I simply hadn't wanted to cloud their thinking with my own diagnosis at that time. And for the longest time, there just never had been the *right* time.

I realized my brother did need to know. I did need to tell him and finally give myself the chance to move on.

Ding. Ding. Ding. Last round.

In May we gathered as a family for a birthday celebration for my brother's daughter. We had just finished dinner and preparations were being made for the cake. As everyone was scattered about the house, I again found myself alone in conversation with my brother. We were discussing how the health issues they had been struggling with within their family had been answered and happily put to rest.

"So what's going on with you? How are you feeling?" he said, pushing me back into the corner.

"I'm fine," I said quickly. "I just have some things I'm dealing with, and now really isn't a good time to talk about it," I finished—a weak attempt at covering up.

"Enough with that already! That's all you keep saying. Why not just tell me what's going on?"

"Fine. Let's go," I said, and motioned for him to go into a private den off of their dining room so that we could discuss this away from the rest of the family.

I entered the room first, followed by my brother who closed the door behind him. I sat down on a bar stool like a boxer in the corner of the ring between rounds, only there wasn't anyone to stand over and coach me for this next round of the fight.—no one to splash water in my face to help me think clearer. There was only my brother, standing behind the bar, waiting for me to stop covering up and come out swinging.

"I have Parkinson's disease. And you can't tell Mom and Dad." Knockout.

CHAPTER 15

MOVED

The great secret of life is the Law of Attraction. That is the main premise in the book, *The Secret* by Rhonda Byrne. It says, that "like attracts like"—when you think a thought, you attract like thoughts to you from the universe. Positive thoughts going out, positive results coming back.

Following that line of thinking, it would only make sense that if your thoughts, deeds and actions shape the person that you are, then those thoughts, deeds and actions will attract similar people to you in the course of your life. In other words, the people that surround you are the closest reflection of you and who you truly are.

If that is the case, then I owe the universe a great deal of thanks for the incredibly flattering compliment it has paid me.

The most amazing and wonderful people in the world surround me. They are members of my family, close friends, coworkers, neighbors and acquaintances. They continually show me their kindness, love, compassion and caring throughout their lives and mine.

I truly am blessed.

During the summer of 2013, the energies, thoughts and vibrations I was sending out into the universe began to undergo a dramatic shift. The change started when I received a brochure in the mail from the National Parkinson Foundation promoting a fundraising walk called Moving Day Chicago. The walk was to be held later in the fall of 2013, on October 20th. The event's mission is threefold: to heighten awareness for Parkinson's

Disease; to promote the positive therapeutic aspects of movement in the lives of Parkinson's patients; and to raise funds for the National Parkinson Foundation.

Now that I was a member of the Parkinson's fraternity (the handshake is a hoot, by the way), I began receiving literature on a very regular basis. Surprisingly, the Parkinson's foundation was outpacing my AARP mailings.

I had actually seen the Moving Day brochure earlier at one of my appointments downtown at the Michael J. Fox PPMI study. Christina had shared it with me as something I might be interested in.

At home, I had tossed the brochure aside, and for a few days it lay amongst the pizza coupons, blacktop services mailings and lawn treatment brochures. My oldest daughter, who happened to be home for a weekend, sat at the kitchen counter, picked it up and started to read it.

"Did you look at this, Dad?" she asked with an enthusiastic tone. "This sounds like fun and like something we should do!"

Was this her sweet way of saying she was worried about me and she wanted to make sure I had commitments to keep me moving so that I didn't end up a Walmart greeter any sooner than my original schedule? Or did my daughter just really want to do something with her Dad? I could have sworn I heard her say "we".

"Sure, Amanda, I'd love to do the walk with you," I replied without hesitation. "What do we need to do?"

Reading from the brochure, she explained that it really was quite simple. First we had to register ourselves as a participating team, and then recruit members to join that team. We needed to pick a team name, designate a team captain, and specify our fundraising goals, both as individuals as well as for our team. We were encouraged to raise funds, but it was not required to participate in the walk. There was no cost whatsoever to sign up.

Easy enough, I thought.

I immediately nominated Amanda as team captain and I also seconded the motion. There were no objections, so she was quickly sworn in. A Moving Day Chicago walk team of two had been formed. Chicago and Parkinson's soon wouldn't know what had hit them.

As the team captain, one of Amanda's first duties was to register our team and both of our team members. After answering all the standard questions of age, sex, contact information and "are you walking in honor of someone with Parkinson's?" or "are you a Parkinson's walker?" we finally got down to the fun stuff.

"We get to pick a team name, Dad."

A sheepish grin came over my face that many of my friends know me well for. It's a look I usually have when my humorous side is coming to the surface, or when the creative, designer's mind is coming to life. When I do advertising work, I love to write the headlines. A headline sets the tone for the entire ad and, if creatively complex enough, can hold multiple meanings at the same time. My brain was churning.

"Maybe it could be a fictitious corporate sponsor: Park n' Sons Pizza! That has possibilities. Or how about a real corporate sponsor: Shakey's Pizza!"

No, it definitely should be connected to what I've told everyone from the beginning. "I'm looking at things on the bright side. If worse comes to worse, I can always get a job with Home Depot as a paint can shaker or at a bar as *a martini shaker.*"

We had our name: "The Martini Shakers." And seeing as it's a fundraiser, we decided our tag line would be, "Working towards a cure from the bottoms up."

After completing all our necessary registration details, Amanda asked me what I felt an achievable fundraising goal was.

"It says, Dad, that for each team member that raises $100, the Foundation awards them a Moving Day Chicago t-shirt on the day of the walk. So we each want to raise at least $100, right?"

I reached higher. "Well, why don't you put yourself down for $250, Amanda, me for $750, and the team goal for $1,000. I feel comfortable that we should be able to raise at least that much."

Little did I realize the impact of the thought I had just put out to the universe. A pebble was dropped in the water and the rings began to grow exponentially, rings that would reach much farther than I would have ever imagined. Like the movement of the tides in the ocean, as the waves go out, they most surely come back to shore. What had left my shore as a soft ripple in the water would return as a wave of love that would knock me over.

CHAPTER 16

THERE IS NOTHING YOU CAN DO

Our efforts for the Moving Day Chicago walk for Parkinson's were now well underway. Our team logo had been designed, and emails had been sent from Amanda and I for what we assumed would be our one and only push toward fundraising.

What happened in that first week of fundraising was nothing short of astonishing. Not only did we each achieve our individual goals of $100 each to receive the Moving Day Chicago t-shirts, but also we achieved *and surpassed* our team goal of $1,000 in just that first week. I honestly was humbled and couldn't believe the response. Donations ranging from $25 to hundreds of dollars were pouring in from close personal friends and former classmates, as well as clients and vendors.

As the weeks went by, we kept readjusting our team goal. One thousand became two thousand, and then two became three. It wasn't long before this new team called The Martini Shakers caught the eye of the Chicago office of the National Parkinson Foundation.

When we first received an email from the Chicago branch director, I wondered if the same sense of humor that consistently got me in trouble in school as the class clown, had done it to me once again. I expected to open the email and read, "We are so happy your team has joined Moving Day Chicago this year, and we look forward to you sharing in the celebration of movement for Parkinson's. But first we have to ask you to change your team name. Take your chair and go sit in the hall, Robert."

To my relief, that wasn't what they said at all; on the contrary. They were very happy we had joined and asked what unique marketing technique we had employed to generate such a fast start in our fundraising. Oh yes, and they closed the email with, "By the way, we love the team name! Very creative."

My email response was simple. There was no unique formula; only the love and caring that the people in my life felt towards this cause.

A direct benefit of our initial fundraising effort was that it made the process of informing friends, clients and neighbors of my PD much easier. I started my letter with, "As some of you are aware of, in July of 2012, I received the diagnosis of Parkinson's disease. I am doing great…" Exposing my diagnosis that way offered me the opportunity to explain how well I was doing with it.

Not long into the campaign, one of my emails to the National Parkinson Foundation caught the attention of the Chicago branch director—more specifically, the *signature* on my emails, which shows I own my own design agency in the Chicago area. The director inquired if I would like to help out with any of the ad design and signage that needed to be done on the local level. I replied that I would be happy to.

As the weeks progressed and our fundraising efforts continued, one unique strategy for raising money did, indeed, begin to emerge—one that I have yet to share with the Foundation.

To fully explain this, I first need to review with you the medications I am taking under the care of Dr. Simuni and the Michael J. Fox PPMI study. The medicine of note is called Neupro. It is a transdermal delivery medication (worn as a patch on the skin) that delivers a 24-hour dose of a dopamine agonist. The drug activates the dopamine receptors in the absence of dopamine in the brain. I must say its positive effect of decreasing my slowness is wonderful.

When Dr. Simuni and Melanie reviewed this drug's precautions with me, I was warned about one possible side effect, and I am repeatedly asked about any symptoms in this regard at every follow up with the study. The side effect was explained an increase in obsessive-compulsiveness and pathological addictions such as gambling, pornography, and hyper-sexuality.

I joked with Melanie, "Well, I'll bet you $100 I won't go back into making sex movies again." She laughed.

While I can say that I've successfully resisted all urges to gamble our life savings away (on what I *know* would be a Parkinson's porno megahit, "Shake That Thang!"), I would eventually discover that I'd developed an obsession for fundraising. Once I started, I found I wanted to do more and more, leading me to believe that what the Foundation ought to do is put all Parkinson's patients on Neupro and turn them loose as fundraisers.

Around the halfway mark of the fundraising timetable, an invitation was sent out to all the team captains inviting them to attend a Moving Day luncheon. The luncheon would serve as a motivational springboard to provide them with strategies for reinvigorating team members toward the final fundraising push. As a result of my involvement on the advertising side, the director extended the invitation to me as well, thinking it would be the perfect opportunity for she and I to meet beyond the exchange of emails.

It's uncanny how the course of events in your life can have a domino effect if you're just open to receiving the message or opportunity. This event was for the purpose of reinvigorating team members and the timing couldn't have been better. I was just one of those that needed the boost.

By this time, the ever-questioning and skeptical side of me had started to slowly creep in. I wanted to make sure that our efforts were going to be fruitful for Parkinson's research, so I read over the literature from the National Parkinson Foundation to remind myself where the funds would be going:

- **Parkinson's disease education and outreach** through public awareness campaigns on early warning signs and treatment, as well as free patient resources for patients and their families
- **Cutting-edge research** aimed at better treatment and care for people with Parkinson's
- **Advancement of clinical care** through healthcare professional training and other initiatives like our Aware in Care program and the Parkinson's disease toolkit
- **Raising awareness**

They did say research, but where *exactly* was the money going? I honestly wasn't sure. I had firsthand knowledge of what the MJF Foundation was doing, as I was a participant in that research.

I put question out to the universe and, unbeknownst to me at the time, the answer came back to me in the form of this luncheon invitation.

By the day of the luncheon, we had increased our team roster by three, recruiting my youngest daughter, Erica, my son, Adam and my wife, Deb. I invited Erica to join Amanda and I for the luncheon downtown.

My daughters and I entered the room where the luncheon was being held and the atmosphere felt immediately welcoming. Sara, the director I had only corresponded with online, immediately recognized me from my picture on the Martini Shakers fundraising page and quickly came over and introduced herself. In fact everyone involved, from local staff to national directors, introduced themselves to us as we took our place at a table.

The room was set up like a small wedding reception with tables of ten scattered about. At the front of the room was a podium with a drop screen and, to the side, a buffet of "Parkinson's appropriate" foods: cold cuts, cheese, pastas and salads—all items you don't have to cut.

Gradually the invitees arrived and the tables began filling up. At our table, informal introductions started to take place. A great majority of the people involved were philanthropic individuals who had known someone with Parkinson's or were spouses or caregivers of a patient. They were now taking on the cause for a loved one. I suddenly had a glimpse of how trying this disease can be on those who care for them.

When it was learned that I was a patient, the focus at our table shifted. Suddenly the conversation became one of, "How are you doing?" and "What are you doing?" Thus began a personal sharing and comparison of experiences. With Parkinson's, all experiences are unique to the individual, and I gathered a sense that everyone is always searching for answers.

I shared with my tablemates the fantastic experience I had been having with the Michael J. Fox Foundation, and how truly blessed I felt to be under the care of such a wonderful staff. And then, as if on cue, as I glanced towards the door, walking in was Dr. Simuni, Melanie, and Karen. With an obvious look of admiration, I announced to my table that the individuals I had just been speaking of were now in attendance.

My foundation care team walked over to our table and we exchanged the same salutation, "What are *you* doing here?" After introducing Dr. Simuni and her staff to my daughters, I shared that we had formed a team of our own and were there for the team captain meeting. Dr. Simuni informed us that the National Parkinson Foundation was the primary contributor on the local level to the research done by the Michael J. Fox Foundation, and that she was there to speak about the research and progress being made.

In that moment I gained all the confirmation I needed to re-energize me for the months of fundraising ahead.

On numerous occasions I have found myself recalling the words of my diagnosing doctor: "There is nothing we can do. We can only treat the symptoms."

There is plenty I can do, I thought to myself.

And our efforts were about to pay dividends ten-fold.

CHAPTER 17

KEEP SMILING

It is often said that a person's eyes are the windows to their soul. If that is true, then their smile must be their soul peering out.

The eyes and smile have long been what immediately attracts me to someone; they are the personal billboards of an individual's character and personality. A *genuine* smile and eyes that have depth, brightness and clarity convey so much—honesty, sincerity, kindness, integrity and trust, just to name a few. As such, they can create an almost immediate sense of comfort for me with that person.

Maybe my propensity to make character assessments in this way comes from my experience art directing photo shoots. As a designer, I have had a number of opportunities to work with both professional models and what we refer to as street talent. Street talent are just what it sounds like—non-professionals that fit the look you're going for, but who can be hired at a substantial discount because they are not working for an agency and have most likely done very little modeling, if any.

Regardless of a model's level of experience, you can quickly learn what a sincere smile and a forced one look like. Manufactured smiles are not unique to just advertising; you run into those same expressions in everyday life as well.

Formulating my impressions this way isn't solely related to my design experience; it's also another product of my intuition. The instinctual message I get from my gut and my heart when I see a warm smile and eyes that engage, allows me to quickly open up and establish that all-important personal connection.

For me, the stronger the personal connection, the greater is the potential for spiritual growth. I would even go so far as to say that I usually feel that intuition simply from viewing a photo; I don't have to have the person present. By just observing those two features, I get most of the initial information I need. As a result, the further along I found myself on my spiritual path and my journey with Parkinson's, the more I began putting that skill to the test.

The first time was during the height of my frustration, when I was trying to determine what was wrong with me medically. I had exhausted all efforts with my internist at the time, and had decided to personally control the direction of my care from then on out. My online search for a neurologist ultimately led me to choose the doctor with the kind smile and compassionate eyes. Within one week of my appointment with her, she made my diagnosis and gave me my answer.

The second was early 2013 after I had settled into my routine with the Northwestern Medical Faculty Foundation and the Michael J. Fox study. I was focusing intently on things I could do to proactively manage my Parkinson's. I had adopted a regular exercise program and was starting to regain some of the tone and muscle I had previously lost. My daily regimen of medicines were giving me back a more normal pace to my movements and I wanted to keep all this positive energy going.

Stress and anxiety can be two of the most destructive components to a Parkinson's patient. I had already seen exactly what it could do to me prior to receiving my diagnosis. My blood pressure was elevated and my breathing was labored. I was experiencing numbness of extremities, headaches, vision problems and sleep disorders. Once I had my diagnosis, I was able to release the anxiety and all of my unrelated symptoms disappeared.

If I wanted to keep my stress and my anxiety in check, I needed to get back to my monthly routine of massage.

My methods for choosing practitioners now seemed to be paying dividends under my new approach, so I decided to employ the same process for finding a new massage therapist.

When I came upon Staci's profile in my search for a masseuse, her resume and credentials were impressive: "A licensed "master" massage therapist serving the holistic health needs of her clients for over sixteen years, with expertise in craniosacral therapy, energy balancing, movement education, neuromuscular massage and shamanic healing".

Parkinson's is a neuro-degenerative disease effecting muscles and movement, two areas of expertise within Staci's profile.

But "shamanic healing"? That sounded...interesting.

I vaguely recalled hearing of shamans before but couldn't recall the specifics. A quick Google of "shaman" yielded a Wikipedia definition that would bring a smile of intrigue to my face.

A shaman, by definition, is a practitioner capable of reaching altered states of consciousness in order to interact with the spirit world and channel transcendental energies into this world. They are regarded as having access to, and influence in, the world of benevolent (friendly) and malevolent (not-so friendly) spirits. They often do so by entering into a trance state during a ritual of healing.

Bingo! I thought. For someone as thirsty for spiritual growth as I was, Staci might just be the shaman I'd been looking for. Plus, her eyes and smile definitely fit the bill.

I promptly scheduled my first appointment with Staci—the first of many to come. Her practice was located within close proximity to my office which made the commute convenient; plus, it was easy to get in a good portion of a day's work before my session.

On the day of my first appointment, while driving from my office to hers, I found myself laughing while thinking about Staci in a trance during the massage. During past experiences I usually found myself to be the one in the trance, quite frequently awakening to an embarrassing snort as I had fallen off to sleep. It struck me as funny to think Staci might be standing there unconscious while I lay there unconscious as well—not much getting done, but two people getting plenty of rest.

That first session and every session since have been anything but ordinary. On the contrary; they have all been extraordinary. Staci is more than a massage therapist. She is a healer, a teacher, an artist and, best of all, a spiritual guide and friend.

From the very beginning, I've often told Staci that I feel I am in my spiritual infancy. Even though I've had a hunger to learn more for over thirty-five years, the questions are as great in number now as they were when I was an inquisitive teen.

The result has been that she has not only rejuvenated my physical energy and helped me manage my Parkinson's symptoms, but she has reenergized my desire to define and understand my spiritual path. I strongly believe the two are going to profoundly change the course of my disease.

One of the first memorable sessions with Staci started as simply as they all do. After arriving at her office and exchanging pleasantries, she would usually inquire about how I was feeling and ask if there were any questions in my heart or tension in my spirit that I would like to have addressed. Something as seemingly simple as this perplexed me in the beginning.

"For example?" I recall asking.

"For example, would you like me to help you work on balance in your life or possibly to achieve greater clarity?" Staci replied with her usual, peaceful demeanor and comforting smile.

"Ah! Now I understand. Given those two choices then, I would say balance. My personal view is that we're always striving for clarity, but I don't think it's something we can ever fully attain."

That's the kind of dialogue I usually engage in with Staci, which I love.

Until this particular massage session, the conversation was usually kept to a minimum or an occasional brief exchange about spirituality. As I laid on the massage table, face down with my head nestled comfortably in the rest, Staci proceeded with her massage. She uses a combination of conventional Swedish massage and craniosacral therapy. For those unfamiliar with CST, there is very little physical pressure and it is more about utilizing "life force energies" to rejuvenate the body. While at times her hands may not be moving, there is an incredible feeling of warmth and energy that passes through you.

It was during a moment like this where her hands were resting on my back, that the silence of the room was softly broken. "There is a man standing next to your left hip right now, and he is wearing a brown coat," Staci softly informed me. I realized immediately she was having a vision.

Her hands now perfectly still on my back, my face still down in the cradle, I calmly asked, "Does he have any discernible features that you can describe for me?"

"Oh yes," she quietly answered. "He is bald. An older man, and he has a very pleasant smile on his face."

"That could very well be my grandfather," I said. "I never had the opportunity to meet him in person, as he had passed away shortly before I was born. He was bald, and everyone in my family said he was always smiling and that he and I were very much alike."

Staci went on to say, "He is now pointing down to your wrist," and I felt Staci's hand touch the friendship bracelet I wore that my youngest daughter had made me years ago.

"Now there is a woman that has joined him. She is small, has short, curly hair that is close to her head and she is wearing librarian-style glasses. She has on a blue flowered dress with an apron tied in front."

"That would be my grandmother," I surmised. "That is exactly how I remember her."

Staci then went on to say, "She's now pointing a finger toward the sky."

And as I lay there contemplating the vision she was painting in my mind, she began to chuckle.

"No, she's not pointing her finger to the sky—she's shaking her finger at him as if she's reprimanding him."

"Now, that is strange that you say that!" I exclaimed to Staci. I explained to her that my brother and I had just spent twelve hours at the hospital recently, waiting as our mom had surgery and recovered. During that wait my brother, who is older and had the opportunity to be acquainted with my grandparent's relationship, had shared with me that our grandmother was not the easiest woman for dear grandfather to live with. She was constantly correcting him or hounding him for something, so he used to escape to the lodge just to get some time away.

And here Staci was describing to me this woman doing just that. At that moment I was convinced that she was seeing my grandparents.

"I've had two opportunities I believe in my life where I had the opportunity to see my grandfather," I confided. "Once in an extremely vivid dream, and again when I had made an appointment for my mom to see a doctor for some nagging pain she'd been having. When the doctor walked in, the man standing there was like every picture I had ever seen of my grandfather. And this man proceeded to fix all of my mom's problems."

"Please tell him thank you for me. That I am thankful he has always been there for me. I've always felt he's been one of my guardian angels. Please tell him thank you," I finished.

"He's smiling now bigger than ever," Staci said.

And I closed my eyes for the rest of the massage.

When the massage was finished not another word was said. Staci left the room and I proceeded to get dressed. I thought about what had just transpired, and what I felt was incredible warmth inside. I had no desire whatsoever to question the event. I wanted it to be what it was. It was special. It was a gift. *Don't be so anxious for the answer, Robert*, I thought to myself. *Enjoy the journey. Enjoy the discovery.*

As I left the room and moved to the entry area, there sat Staci, finishing a small painting. She turned to me and said, "I painted this for you."

On a 6-inch square of watercolor paper was a blue circle, which worked its way around the paper from deep blue to light blue at the end of the stroke. The circle was open at one side. In the center of the circle was a lavender heart. It was simple, yet beautiful. Prophetically, it would be the first of many times to come that a blue circle would appear in my life.

"Thank you," I said, "And thank you for sharing your vision with me as well."

"You're very welcome," she humbly replied.

I left with the painting and headed home.

That night as I lay down into bed, I thought about the opportunity I had just been given as a gift. I kept thinking about Staci saying how my grandfather was smiling and, in my mind, I could picture that smile that I'd seen in so many photographs of him before. Although I had never had the opportunity to see his smile in person, I never doubted the sincerity or kindness of the man behind that smile. His smile was real. He was genuinely happy.

And so was I.

CHAPTER 18

STRENGTH IN NUMBERS

July 12th, 2013, would mark the one-year anniversary of my diagnosis of Parkinson's disease. It would also be the date when The Martini Shakers would reach $4,000 in fundraising for the Moving Day Chicago walk.

It was wonderful to be able to experience the positive effects that can come out of something so seemingly negative. Our fundraising results had not only been positive, but they had already grown beyond our expectations. We had quadrupled our initial goal of $1,000. We could have very easily been satisfied with what we had accomplished and become complacent until the walk on October 20th, but I knew we could do more. We just had to get creative.

While growing up, I always had a job. I enjoyed having money and I liked to be able to buy myself things, like saving for and buying my very first car at the age of sixteen.

My mom used to say, "Bob, you have champagne taste on a beer budget," which, to me, meant she saw me wanting to live way beyond my means. I also understood she was trying to teach me that happiness and fulfillment don't necessarily come from the things you can buy or how much money you have. I know she was reinforcing good values in me.

To me, that drive to want to provide more for myself wasn't a bad thing at all. It was a force behind the early development of my creativity. Not artistic creativity, mind you, but the kind of creativity that assists someone in surviving financially. I always felt there wasn't a job I couldn't do, if someone would be willing to simply take the time to show me.

There were the jobs I'd had that didn't require any extensive training at all, like delivering the Champaign News Gazette newspaper while in college at the University of Illinois in Urbana-Champaign. That job required waking up each morning at 5 a.m. to roll and rubber band the stacks of newspapers that had been dropped at my apartment door. I'd walk my route in the dark, flinging newspapers onto porches or stuffing them into mailboxes. Little did I know at the time how much that job would be preparing me for life.

Just six years later I began working for a computer gaming software company called Mindscape, Inc., where I would design the packaging for the computer version of the popular arcade hit, Paperboy. In this game, the object was to earn the most points by slinging newspapers while avoiding free-roaming dogs.

Leap forward some twenty-five years to 2013 and my need for a new way to fundraise for the Moving Day walk. At this point, I had pretty much exhausted my list of everyone I knew personally. I had reached out to every friend I had contact information for, along with clients, colleagues and vendors that I was either doing business with or had done business with. There wasn't an individual I personally knew that I had left to contact.

So why not contact the people I don't know?

I immediately put my design skills to use. I drafted a flyer that introduced myself to the community and explained my cause. I was honest and open, and I shared the personal story of my diagnosis, much like I am doing now. More importantly, I explained my commitment to this cause and I asked them to share in that commitment, if not directly for me, then maybe for someone they loved or knew who had also been effected by this disease. I explained that we were going to be producing t-shirts with our team logo printed on them, and for a $25 donation we would add the name of someone they wanted to sponsor to our shirt; for a $50 donation, we would provide them with a shirt as well.

I printed three hundred flyers.

Each night I would sit in our bedroom to roll and rubber band the flyers just like I had prepared newspapers for delivery in college. At 5 a.m. the next morning, I would fill up a bag with my flyers and begin walking our subdivision in the dark. One by one, I canvassed some three hundred homes in our development placing my flyer by the flag of the homeowner's mailbox.

To be out walking at that time of the morning as everyone slept was meditative. It was actually quite energizing. I'd focus on the positive aspects of my life, the people and events that had brought me to where I was, and I'd give thanks for everyone who had supported me in this cause. I was drawing strength and comfort from my sincere belief that there is a purpose for this experience and everything yet to come.

I knew firsthand, from all the years I had worked in marketing and advertising, that if I received a two- to three-percent response on my direct mail piece, I would have met the industry average. So of my three hundred flyers, if I heard from six to nine people, I would have done ok. That would equate my efforts to total donations of perhaps $150 to $450.

We took in $3,125. So much for averages when you're marketing to the universe.

The donations were coming in, in a variety of amounts, for a variety of purposes. Twenty-five dollars in the name of a beloved uncle. Fifty dollars because they just felt it was wonderful what we were doing. Fifty to honor the husband of a co-worker who was also living with the disease. One hundred for 2 t-shirts from a couple that just felt blessed with their good health. All the while, I was taking note of individuals we would be honoring and t-shirts to be delivered.

The most humbling moment came, however, when a neighborhood gentleman who had received the flyer called and said he wanted to stop by with a check. It wasn't long after I hung up the phone, that he pulled his vehicle into our driveway. We watched as he slowly stepped out and started a slow and arduous walk to our front door.

He explained that six months earlier, he had suffered a stroke, leaving him for a good period of time with minimal use of his left side. Months of intense and painful rehabilitation had returned him to this miraculous state of being able to drive over and walk up to our house. His beautiful wife is living with Multiple Sclerosis. They are a couple that most might agree have every right to be more concerned with their own health and financial needs than concerning themselves with another person's cause. But he is a soul that understands that connection we all hold. He chose to make the donation from his heart, not because he was expected to, but because he wanted to. He wanted to be a part of a good thing.

He reached into his pocket and handed me a check.

It read $1,000. I was speechless.

We were a month away from the October walk date, and our fundraising had brought in well over $8,000 in donations. That ripple we had sent out into the universe was now a wave crashing on shore.

When I first received my diagnosis of Parkinson's, a strange sense of relief and calm came over me. The long period of "not knowing" what was ailing me had actually been more frightening than having the answer. Finally having the knowledge of what it was gave me the opportunity to define its place in my life, and allowed me the opportunity to deal with it in my own way.

My intuition has served me well and tells me everything will be all right. I feel confident that I cannot only manage the disease but, with positive thoughts and attitudes that I draw from my spirituality, I can conquer it. I decided early on I was going to take an active role in research, empowerment and increasing awareness about Parkinson's. I knew I needed to stand up to this disease as opposed to just sitting back and letting be what will be.

I realize that, early on, I had overlooked a crucial ally in my fight. My main focus had been on what *I* needed to do to effectively manage my health, all the while neglecting to acknowledge the universe of powerful positive energy that wanted to work with me on my behalf. Regardless of the approach I take, I know I will always have the support and love of my family. But the Moving Day walk and the outpouring of support from all of those friends and strangers reaffirmed to me that I am not alone in this fight. I have a universe of energy I can bring to bear against it. They are my family, my friends, my acquaintances and the strangers in my life that respond to the vibrations going out.

They are the like attracted by like.

I have strength in numbers.

CHAPTER 19

O2

Take a slow, deep breath. Try and be very conscious of how the breath feels in your lungs all the way through as you slowly inhale and then slowly exhale.

Go ahead. Try it.

Try it a couple of times and *really* pay attention to every part of the breath.

It starts with the beginning of the breath where your lungs slowly fill like the start of a roller coaster ride. You can almost imagine the breath climbing higher and higher inside you until it begins to slow and your lungs are filled to capacity. Then, when you reach the very top of the breath where you can't take in any more air, you can actually feel yourself coming over the top of the roller coaster and starting the descent downward, exhaling as you go.

There is a small magical moment in that life-sustaining cycle—a point that epitomizes complete satiation. That moment is just past the very top of the breath when you are just beginning to exhale. To me, it symbolizes taking in all of the energy your world has to offer, feeling that satiation and exhaling your statement of content to the universe. It is bliss.

That is what a massage, from a master massage therapist, a shaman, a teacher, a healer is like.

My last massage appointment with Staci offered another glimpse of her talent. Not only did I leave reenergized in both body and spirit, she had shared with me her vision of the spirits that are an integral part of my life.

She offered me confirmation of what I had long believed in my heart, that there are energies at play all around us that shape and guide us through this journey of life. She rejuvenated my spiritual intuition.

Upon leaving that appointment, Staci presented me with a small painting, saying that often right after a vision during a session, she may feel the desire to paint. She painted it in the few minutes it took me to get ready.

It takes me longer than that just to pick out a tie.

To say I had been anxious for my next massage session with Staci would be a monumental understatement. The effects in relation to my Parkinson's were already noticeable to me. Our sessions gave me a new level of energy in my workouts and in my day. As for stress relief, well, let's just say I learned to use that deep breath, over and over and over.

So during our next session, in the midst of our conversations, I had to inquire about the painting. While lying on my stomach, I lifted my head from the rest and asked, "What about the painting you painted for me last session—what did it mean? What inspired your vision?"

Her answer was not what I had expected.

"You'll have to forgive me. When I paint after a vision, I'm often still in such a state that I don't always recall what I painted."

"Really?" I said with disappointment in my voice.

For the past three weeks, learning the meaning of the circle and heart had occupied my thoughts. I had battled my personal weakness of wanting the answer quickly as opposed to enjoying the journey and discovery. I thought for sure Staci held the answer for me. *You're a shaman*, I thought to myself.

"It was a blue circle that started from a deep blue and slowly faded to a light blue until the brush was out of ink. It was open on one side. And in the center was a lavender heart that was deeper in tone at its center," I described with a wide-eyed expression. "Remember?"

She smiled at me and said, "I'm sorry. I don't recall. I don't always know the meaning behind the things I share. Sometimes I do, but at other times it's for the client to interpret."

"What does it mean to you, Robert?" she asked.

I laid my head back down on the headrest and stared at the floor, thinking that maybe the answer might appear to me.

Unfortunately, the only blue circle that would appear was the one around my face when I turned over to lie on my back. I swear, my head always feels like it has a hundred pounds in it when it presses down into that face rest. Yet, when put to the test with a question like *what does the blue circle and heart mean to me*, I realized there wasn't much in my head after all.

I pondered for a while. "Maybe the blue represents my universe, and the heart represents the center of my intuition and how I relate to my universe. And the opening in the circle represents my need to send more energy out and to allow more energy in." I looked at her like I had just tried to bluff my way through a physics problem on a chalkboard.

Even I didn't buy that one.

However, I was eager to learn, and who better to learn from than the master herself?

I had already expressed my interest to Staci in attending a seminar she was conducting with another shamanic energy practitioner named Bridget on *Intuitive Tracking*. It centered on the idea that we all possess an inner wisdom, an "intuitive compass", meant to help guide us through our lives. The seminar would help us tap into this inner wisdom and learn how to use it to make more dynamic, empowered choices in our relationships, careers, and other areas of our life.

I already felt that I had a strong intuitive base that I had been using in making some of the decisions regarding my Parkinson's. Sharpening my skills certainly couldn't hurt. And besides, it might actually be fun.

I registered to participate in this seminar on a Saturday morning. Registration was limited to twelve people so that it would be an intimate opportunity to learn and share.

Bridget, Staci's partner in the seminar, was also a yoga instructor, so we were asked to bring a yoga mat along as we would be doing some beginner level yoga in addition to some of the other activities planned. I was elated to hear it was beginner level, because I had never tried yoga in my life. The only Downward Dog I was familiar with was with our Golden Retriever, and I was certain it wouldn't be like that (though treats certainly would have been welcomed on my part).

We were also asked to prepare for the seminar by bringing with us a question or an internal tension we were carrying that we would like to find clarity or resolution with. By coming to the seminar, you agreed to leave all ego aside and be willing to be open and vulnerable in order to make progress. Everything shared of a personal nature would remain in the confidence of that day—sort of a what-happens-at-the-shaman-seminar-stays-at the-shaman-seminar agreement Fine by me.

Maybe I could get over my fear of sharing my life story to the public. (That's a joke for my wife.)

Seminar Saturday finally arrived. Grabbing my morning cup of coffee, I was on my way. I'd neglected to bring a yoga mat, not only because I didn't have one, but because I wasn't planning to take up yoga anytime soon (although yoga is definitely known to promote positive health results for Parkinson's patients). I figured I should be comfortable enough on the carpet.

As I entered the building, Bridget greeted me. I recognized her immediately because I had done my due diligence. As I always do in my business, I research someone I will be meeting with to know his or her philosophy of business or background.

"Good morning, Robert! It's nice to finally meet you. I'm glad you could attend," she said as she reached out and shook my hand.

"Good morning, Bridget," I responded while wondering, *How did she know my name? Has she also gone to the effort of looking up each attendee so she could recognize us by face as we arrived? Or did she simply hear my name in a moment of clairvoyance?*

Perhaps I was simply the last to arrive and, by process of elimination, the only attendee left was "Robert".

As if she heard the dialogue in my head, she smiled at me and said, "We're still waiting for the majority of the attendees to arrive, so please go downstairs to the classroom and make yourself comfortable. Staci and I will be down shortly."

Wow, she's good, I thought to myself. *This is going to be fun.*

I made my way downstairs to a small room with rolled up yoga mats placed in a semi circle on the floor. *Hey, that worked out well,* I thought to myself. Maybe my intuition had kicked in already. The room was softly lit and some candles were burning for ambiance—a nice feng shui atmosphere.

There were two women who had already arrived, so I sat down on one of the yoga mats and introduced myself. Gradually, more and more people arrived until the room was filled with our expected group of twelve.

There's always the potential for that awkward silence when a group of people who don't know each other are put together in a room. Like going to a traffic school class after receiving a ticket, you sit there taking in the faces of everyone else, gauging their hesitancy about being there, their level of shyness or outgoingness. I love people watching. It's intuitive tracking, in essence, which we were here to hone our skills on. However, in an intimate setting such as this, it's simply like a group of twelve, sitting on yoga mats in an elevator with no floor numbers to look at. The silence was deafening.

So as Bridget and Staci walked in, I figured someone had to break the tension and I just knew the one to do it ("*Robert, do you want to take your chair to the hall?*" I heard in my head).

"I must say, Bridget, when I first arrived upstairs, I was completely mesmerized by your ability to know me by my first name. I thought to myself, *Wow, this woman has a remarkable gift. We had never seen each other before and yet she knows who I am out of a group of twelve. She's clairvoyant.* Then as the other eleven attendees arrived, I had to laugh at myself when the answer to your magic became clear."

What I neglected to mention to this point, is that the remaining nine individuals who arrived were all women. Rounding out the group with Staci and Bridget, our intimate gathering was now made up of thirteen women and myself.

"I'm looking forward to being mesmerized again," I finished, as the other ladies chuckled.

Not only would I be mesmerized; I was about to be blown away.

After going around the group introducing ourselves and sharing the individual question we each held for ourselves, we unrolled our yoga mats. We did some cleansing breaths for clearing the mind, along with some basic yoga poses for preparing our bodies. I quickly learned all my core work at home was nothing compared to what a yoga routine could do for me. My core was shaking as if every Parkinson's tremor I might have in my body suddenly migrated to my abdomen. My bridge pose looked like a Tickle Me Elmo doll gone berserk.

We were taught about the seven chakras within our bodies, the centers through which all energy flows. We learned how to open them, cleanse them of negative energy and close them. We also learned how to read our own chakras, putting our own questions to ourselves and allowing the answers to come.

Once we had prepared our minds and our bodies, and Staci had shared the basic concept behind "intuitive tracking", we were asked to pair up with one person in the group that we did not know. The fact that I did not know anyone opened up the entire group as a possibility for me. As I began to scan the group, one woman immediately spoke up and said, "Robert, I'd like to work with you."

"Great." I said, "Joyce, right?" which she acknowledged with a smile and a nod of her head. I was proud of myself. In the past I've been one to forget someone's first name after five minutes of the introduction, but my recall of the eleven ladies' names in our group was remarkably good. Maybe all that word quizzing with Christina in the Michael J. Fox PPMI study was paying dividends.

After shuffling everyone around to pair up, we were given our instructions for the lesson on tracking. We were to decide who would go first, and that person would be the "reader", while the other person was simply to be observed. We agreed that Joyce would be the first to be observed, and that I would be the reader. The observed was instructed to, again, state their question or issue they want to have tracked, and basically just stand in front of the person reading them.

The reader was then instructed to open their mind to receiving information by taking a cleansing breath and clearing their mind. Next, we were to mentally work through each of the seven chakras of the other person, gathering the information we received from each chakra. We were to be mindful to try not to filter, edit, analyze or judge the information we received. We could ask them to hold our hands if we wanted, or we could even close our own eyes. The idea was to simply be open and receptive to that person's energy.

We each had a notepad and were instructed to write down ANYTHING that came to us: A feeling. A thought. A vision. A sound. There were no right things or wrong things. Just observe and take note.

After ten minutes, we were to review with each other what we observed and, after asking permission of that person, share those impressions with the group.

Now I have to admit, and I told Staci as much at our next massage appointment, that I felt disappointed. I felt I had failed. I anticipated that the information I'd receive would come to me much like the "hit" I'd experienced walking down that street in Milwaukee, where as clear as could be, a vision just popped in my head—but it didn't. I sat there empty.

I did observe Joyce and I felt impressions of who she is, just like I do when I see a person's smile and eyes. I saw kindness, shyness, confidence and hesitancy, *All surface characteristics*, I thought to myself. *But nothing that answers her personal question or issue.* I shared all of this with Joyce—all except one strange vision I had of a small white dog by her right shoulder, which felt made up and irrelevant, so I didn't mention it. By neglecting that, I truly did fail; I judged my own thoughts.

To this day I wonder if the white dog might have meant anything to her.

Next it was my turn to stand and be observed. For ten minutes I stood in front of Joyce, as she diligently looked me over. In design school and throughout my career, I have often stood in front of the class or a client as they critiqued my work, so I wasn't a stranger to putting myself in front of someone, but this was a little different.

Joyce was writing feverishly which gave me the impression she was getting much more from me than I had gotten from her. She finished her notes and I sat down in front of her as she asked me if she could share what she saw.

"Absolutely," I agreed, feeling both anxious and apprehensive at the same time.

Starting with my base chakra and working her way up through all seven, she shared with me everything she observed or perceived.

"At your base chakra, which represents your foundation, I felt a sense of instability, not threatening to your prosperity, but somehow your balance is being disturbed."

That's very interesting that she senses something off with my balance, I thought, since I hadn't shared with this group anything about my Parkinson's diagnosis.

Joyce continued to work her way upward through my remaining chakras, describing how she was marveling at the colors she perceived. She saw bright blues in my mid chakras that became brighter and brighter as she continued upward. When she reached my crown chakra, she described it as a shower of golden light that came cascading down over my being, which ultimately aided in stabilizing my foundation.

Wow, I thought. *She did much better than I did.*

But she wasn't done. She went on to describe, "There was one very strange vision that appeared on it's own, that I honestly don't know what it means. As I looked at you, I suddenly had a vision of a blue circle encompassing your whole body."

"A blue circle?" I asked, with a look of astonishment on my face.

"Yes. A blue circle was all around you."

My head immediately snapped to the right to where I knew Staci was standing over at the side of the room. She had been observing all the pairings, only when I looked over, she was looking right at me. She had been listening to our conversation.

My look said it all, and I knew she had heard what Joyce had just shared, so my abbreviated statement was understood with full clarity. "Come on! A blue circle?"

Staci smiled at me briefly, and then calmly said, "It's not my read," which obviously meant that it was my time with Joyce and therefore her observation, not Staci's.

I felt chills run up my spine and Joyce saw the look of bewilderment on my face. I briefly wondered if Joyce was somehow part of an elaborate game, but I was really more in awe of her having done so well.

"You're good," was all I could say.

I took a deep breath.

CHAPTER 20

REMEMBERING TO FORGET

One of the most difficult struggles I've had with my Parkinson's disease is forgetfulness.

I'm not referring to the kind of memory lapses like forgetting where I put my keys or where one of my fifty pairs of reading glasses are located (usually one pair is on top of my head). Nor trying to recall which of my daughters was born on the 2nd of March and which one was born on the 18th. And I'm not referring to the onset of dementia, which is a distinct possibility for a PD patient. No, the type of forgetfulness I am talking about is forgetting about my Parkinson's disease itself.

Don't get me wrong—from the very first day of my diagnosis, not a day has gone by that "Parkinson's" has not crossed my mind.

I would venture to guess that most Parkinson's patients, like myself, are also in the constant state of self-evaluation and awareness. There is a variety of daily symptoms ready to remind even the most easily distracted of individuals: lightheadedness while up and about; stiffness in the hands and fingers that cause a loss in dexterity; skin rash from repeated applications of the medication patch; sleep disturbances; a hoarse voice; and a generalized all-over slowness.

The morning self-evaluation is my personal guide for anticipating what my day might be like. Regardless of my medications being 24-hour extended-release, there is still a sense of being "on" or "off", depending on how effective the medicine feels at any given time, so I plan my appointments and activities accordingly.

As much as a Parkinson's patient may try and not think about their disease, and go about their life as if everything is normal, there just simply is no way to deny it. I am sure there are friends, acquaintances and family of mine who wish I could forget about it, too. Ever since my diagnosis, they have been inundated with reminders of my Parkinson's on almost a daily basis through my obsessive involvement in fundraising, building awareness, blogging and writing. To those people, I'd like to say thank you for your understanding.

As much as I wish I could go about each day without physical reminders of my disease, where a slowness in my movement or a stumble on the carpet would be overlooked by my brain, just like an itch on my nose or a sneeze, I consciously choose not to forget about Parkinson's itself.

Yes, I have everyday physical reminders that tap me on the shoulder so that I will never forget I have this disease. But rather than allowing those limitations to remind me of what Parkinson's is doing to me, I choose to remember I have the opportunity I've been given to fight against it—for myself and for others.

Chapter 21

Flip Flops

With less than one month before the National Parkinson Foundation's Moving Day Chicago walk to benefit Parkinson's, our team, The Martini Shakers, was preparing for one final push in our fundraising efforts.

For the vast majority of our four-month campaign, we had maintained a position in the top four of the 120-plus other teams who were actively fundraising for the walk. Of those top four teams, we were the only one that did not have a corporate matching sponsorship, so we felt a great deal of pride in what our supporters had allowed us to accomplish to date.

Not only were we achieving new milestones in fundraising for our team, but we were forging new friendships as well. One result of my early-morning neighborhood mailbox-stuffing, was a donation made in honor of a coworker's spouse who had been diagnosed with Parkinson's disease. The very next day I received an email from a woman who said that she was that coworker, and that she had just been informed that the donation had been made in her husband's honor. She went on to say that she and her husband would love to join our team if it was not too late. She told me her husband was close to my age and had also been recently diagnosed with PD, but he hadn't been taking things as positively as I appeared to be. She felt that an opportunity for him to meet me and discuss our similar situations might be of some help to him.

I said, "Absolutely, we would be honored to have you both on our team. And as a matter of fact, we have a fundraiser coming up that we would love for you to be a part of."

My oldest daughter Amanda, our team captain, with the help of her boyfriend Dave and his family, were busy organizing a benefit party and raffle to be held at a local bar. It was billed as the Party for Parkinson's, and would be complete with a live DJ, raffles for a variety of Chicago area sports items such as Chicago Blackhawks tickets, apparel and merchandise; Chicago Bears and Chicago Bulls gift baskets; and additional donated items. They literally were putting the event together in a matter of weeks.

The establishment, Flip Flops Tiki Bar and Grill, could not have been more accommodating or instrumental in making the benefit such a huge success. They donated "Shaker Shots" which we sold to raise additional revenue; an authentic Chicago Blackhawks jersey for our raffle; and their wait staff's services for the entire event.

Invitations were sent out to friends and acquaintances, and signs were posted at the bar to attract local patrons as well. The turnout was fantastic. Through raffle ticket, Shaker Shots and t-shirt sales that evening, we took in an additional $2,000, bringing our total to over $12,000 with just one week left.

Our final fundraising tally was an amazing $13,703, an astonishing accomplishment from an initial goal set at just $1,000.

The whole fundraising process was an incredibly humbling experience, to witness such an outpouring of love and support from family, friends, acquaintances, and strangers alike, which ultimately culminated with the Moving Day walk on October 20th, 2013.

However, the five months of fundraising and final event festivities would surprisingly come at a heavy emotional cost for me.

My father is eighty-six years old. He has survived a quintuple bypass surgery, had a pacemaker implant, and a staff infection around his aorta that required a seven-hour surgery. He has high blood pressure, high cholesterol and diabetes. Having outlived his father by twenty-eight years, my father is truly a living testament to the miracles of modern medicine—that, and my mother's prayers.

My mother is seventy-eight and has raised two sons She has dealt with pancreatitis, high blood pressure and high cholesterol, and has lived with severe back pain for the major portion of her life. Recently, she underwent surgery for an esophageal hernia that repaired a ten-inch hole in her diaphragm to keep her stomach from protruding into her esophagus (making it impossible for her to keep food down).

To say that my parents have been through a lot medically and could be considered in fragile health at their age would be quite an understatement. My car, which has over 170,000 miles on it, is in the shop for repairs less than my mom and dad.

My parent's health and age played a major role in my decision early on not to share my Parkinson's disease diagnosis with them. I simply couldn't see anything positive come from telling them. So after much consideration, internal debate, strong negative response from my son, and less than supportive responses from the rest of my family, I had made my decision and had asked everyone to please respect my wishes and, in essence, be a part of my ruse.

For the next year-and-a-half, no mention would be made of my Parkinson's disease during family birthday parties or holiday gatherings. There was no discussion when I drove my mother to the Northwestern Medical Faculty Foundation for her appointment with her new hernia doctor, even though it was in the same building I visited on a regular basis for the Michael J. Fox Foundation PPMI study. There was no mention made during the countless times she would call my office and ask why I sounded so tired on the phone. No mention was ever made by anyone in the family on the evening of the Party for Parkinson's, or the day of the NPF's Moving Day Chicago walk, the two events at which every member of our family, except for my parents, were in attendance.

I had just wanted to spare my parents the worry. I simply couldn't fathom how giving them that burden could enhance the quality of their life, or mine for that matter. I needed to define what place Parkinson's would occupy in my life before my mom tried to define it as all of my life. My doctors had already explained, "There is nothing we can do." Well, I certainly knew there was nothing my mom and dad could do.

I soon learned that I couldn't have been more wrong.

These were the two people who had sat through countless little league baseball games from the time I was six years old until I was well into high school. They were always in the stands to cheer me on for my accomplishments—like when I pitched a no-hitter—and they were also there to cheer for me when I walked back to the dug out after striking out.

They attended band concerts, choir concerts, plays and operettas, always the first to put a hand on my shoulder and say, "We're so proud of you. You did great."

And they were there for all my failures too, with a hug and a smile. They never questioned me when I decided to change majors from Aviation to Art & Design, in essence starting my college education all over; on the contrary. They said, "You'll do great at whatever you set your mind to." Because that's what parents do. At least that's what my parents did. They were always there to support me in any endeavor I undertook—every endeavor except this one, my fight against Parkinson's.

I had denied them that opportunity and, in doing so, had just proven the theory behind the book, *The Secret*, which says your positive or negative thoughts bring back to you more of the same.

In essence, my effort to save my parents from any hurt, brought the hurt right back to myself. The thought I put out into my universe was: *I don't want to feel guilty by hurting my parents with the news of my diagnosis.* But whether I prefaced it with "want" or "don't want", the essence of the thought was my *intent*—in my case, "feel guilty".

So that is exactly what I received in return. Guilt.

While I was completely overwhelmed, humbled and appreciative of the outpouring of support that came, not only in the form of monetary donations but in written expressions of love and concern as well, the incredible turnouts at both the Party for Parkinson's and the Moving Day Chicago walk still left me with a sense of emptiness. Of all the truly genuine, heart-felt displays of support that had been offered, the two individuals that I knew in my heart would most want to be encouraging, "We're so proud of what you've done—you'll do great with this fight," weren't allowed to be part of it. It just wasn't complete.

I decided then and there that if I was going to move forward successfully in this fight, I needed to add two more people to my team. The time had come to tell my parents.

CHAPTER 22

SHAKE A LEG

My first recollection of deceiving my parents was around the age of five when, in the thralls of a pillow fight with my older brother and our babysitter, we busted a clock on the mantle. Frankly, the pillow fight would have made Braveheart proud. However, I doubt that after any of his conquests he ever tried to glue one of his victims back together. Needless to say, we did—and we got caught. My brother and I neglected to realize two key details. One, the glues of the day didn't work on glass, and two, that the clocks of the day needed to be wound regularly. The first time my father went to wind it, it fell apart in his hands.

It wouldn't surprise me if there had been an even earlier time, when my parents were trying to potty-train their toddler. I can just picture myself standing there, vehemently denying having made a mess in my diaper, all the while not realizing that the "cologne" I was wearing had given me away. But I was too young to remember, so that doesn't count. Suffice it to say, I started deceiving my parents early on, and apparently I have continued that tradition into the present.

We had just completed the Moving Day Chicago walk for Parkinson's at the end of October, so Thanksgiving was looming on the horizon. If I was going to stay committed to my decision to tell my parents of my PD diagnosis, then I had to follow through with it as soon as possible.

My wife and I have hosted Thanksgiving every year for over twenty-five years and we always include both sides of the family. Assuming that my parents would need time to adjust to my news, I want to give them as much time as possible, rather than having them come to the dinner with raw emotions. I imagined my wife at the Thanksgiving table saying, "Bob, could you please *shake* up the can of whip cream for the pumpkin pie?", followed by a wail of grief from my mother.

As I have mentioned, the most adamant opposition to my parental deception came from my son Adam. All along he kept saying, "How would you feel if it was one of your children not telling you?" So when my decision was made to fess up, there couldn't have been a stauncher supporter. To Adam, though, the day couldn't come soon enough.

Now, my son Adam is a very unique young man. He truly is blessed with a heart and soul full of love, and his every thought comes from kindness and caring. He is extremely empathetic and is always thinking of others' feelings. As such, he has always loved going to spend a weekend with my parents. Even as a sixteen-year-old, an age when most teenagers are scrambling to spend time with their friends, my son would gladly spend a weekend with his grandma and grandpa just because, as he says, "They don't have anyone else to keep them company. They're lonely. And I like being with them." He has a heart of gold and is an old soul beyond his years.

We set a date for Adam to spend the weekend with my parents, and discussed that we would tell them my news when we dropped him off to stay. Adam liked the idea, especially because he said he would be able to help them with any concerns or questions they had once the rest of the family had left.

I couldn't have been more nervous that day. Before we left to drive to my parents, we informed the girls of our plan. My oldest, Amanda, advised that I should do it like ripping off a Band-Aid, not slow and dragged out like she said I had told them almost a year ago. Certainly not as slowly as I gave my speech at the Party for Parkinson's, when Amanda had given me the "out of time" signal, miming a cutting motion across her throat. (Moments later when I had asked why she had been giving me that sign, she replied, "The Chicago Blackhawks game was coming back on, Dad! You needed to stop talking.")

Wow. Where's my team captain now?

As we drove to my parent's house, I felt it necessary to go over my plan aloud, knowing full well that Adam was going to be very anxious for me to come clean. To him, this was my penance for having kept it from them for so long. I believe that a part of him enjoyed seeing me on the hot seat. He was looking forward to this.

"Now Adam, I don't want you to anticipate that I am just going to walk into their house and tell them right away. I can't. I want to sit and talk to them for a while and I don't want you saying anything like, 'Dad, don't you have something you want to say?'. OK?"

He quickly retorted, "Sure, what's a little longer. I won't say anything."
Heart of gold.

I was going to my parents' house armed like a vacuum cleaner salesman from the 1940s. With me was an arsenal of literature: brochures from the National Parkinson Foundation; informational collateral from Northwestern Medical Faculty Foundation; and my trump card, the Good Housekeeping magazine interview with Michael J. Fox. No one can ever be sad looking at Michael.

Put out positive thoughts. Now is the time to put it to use.

It was amazing how nervous and concerned for their well being I was. *Should I program 911 into my phone? Oh, that's stupid,* I immediately thought as I actually laughed at myself. *But do I know my parents' address in case I need to call an ambulance?* I'd be sure and take note of it as we pulled in the drive.

Annnnd...we were there. *OK. Deep breath. Just rip the Band-Aid right off.*

My parents live in a small, two-bedroom town home with one-and-a-half baths and two levels. The layout wasn't a problem years ago when they moved in, but now a chair lift adorns the staircase. Because my dad periodically loses his balance, his doctor suggested they install one. And when he uses it, we ask him to hold an umbrella so we can sing Mary Poppins songs.

The living room has a large sofa and adjacent love seat, which overlook a small dining area. Their TV sits in the dining area so that, regardless of where they are sitting, they can watch their shows—the news, the Bulls, the Hawks, and reruns of The Match Game.

We arrived during a Bulls game, so it was easy to start with some small talk. "Derek Rose is looking good. Let's hope he doesn't get hurt this season," I said to my dad, not realizing the thought I had just put out in the universe.

We continued to chat for ten to fifteen minutes and Adam had, indeed, not said a word—with his mouth. His eyes, however, were another story entirely. He paced back and forth from living room to dining room, while glaring at me with the subtlety of a mime trapped in an imaginary box, as if to say, "Well? When are you going to say something?" You couldn't miss him. He was an albatross.

Finally my mother spoke up. "What's wrong with Adam?" to which I replied, "Oh, there's something he's been wanting me to tell you."

I searched for the edge of the Band-Aid to grab a hold of.

"First, I owe you and Dad an apology for not having told you this a while ago." My mom's expression went somber. My heart sank. But I stayed positive.

"Almost a year-and-a-half ago I was diagnosed with Parkinson's disease. But I'm really doing great. I promise you."

And like the cute salt and pepper shakers that they are to me, my father, sitting next to my mother, turned to her and said, "What did he say?"

"He has Parkinson's disease," my mom repeated and, to my surprise, she was stoic. They both were. The mother and father I had feared telling because I thought they couldn't take it, sat there as calmly as could be, listening to me explain every detail. In that one sitting, I told them most everything I have shared here up to this point. We talked about the diagnosis, the treatments, and my involvement in the MJF Foundation PPMI Study, the Party for Parkinson's and the Moving Day Chicago walk.

But there was a surprise reaction, truly one I never expected. "Alright, already! Gee, how long are you going to go on? I thought you were just going to tell them you had Parkinson's, not tell them your life story! Aren't you two going out tonight? Go, already!"

Adam. *Heart of gold.*

CHAPTER 23

WEE OOH

"Sometimes your joy is the source of your smile, but sometimes your smile can be the source of your joy." ~ Thích Nhất Hạnh

Like most kids growing up, I had a variety of pets: dogs, birds and fish, mostly. I did have a pet squirrel, too, although Petey didn't live with us. My parents felt that pets taught responsibility. A pet required love and care. So as a result I always felt a special connection to animals. I mean, I wouldn't refer to myself as a horse whisperer or a Dr. Dolittle, but I always had empathy for animals and believed that they possessed a spiritual essence.

Take, for example, every time my children have asked me to kill a spider on their wall. After having brought the bug to its demise, I would announce, in my best tiny spider voice, "Well, I guess Daddy Spider won't be bringing dinner home for his children tonight," as I would sadly flush it down the toilet.

I simply want to teach my children compassion for all living things.

I will admit my level of compassion for animals might seem extreme to some.

Like when I was seven years old and cleaning my fish aquarium. The usual procedure was to take a plastic baggie, fill it with some of the water from the tank, catch your fish and put them in the bag, then empty the tank, clean it and prepare it with fresh water. It's no problem, as long as your knot on the baggie is tight when you set it in the bathroom sink—or at the very least, you close the stopper in the sink. I had neglected to do either one correctly. I insisted that my father could not shave for a week, for fear of scalding my fish to death.

Or at the age of nine, when my parakeet had a heart attack and I found him belly-up on the bottom of his cage, but still showing signs of life. In the middle of the night, I called our veterinarian to get emergency instruction on Budgie CPR. I followed his directions methodically: Mix two parts of honey with two parts of whiskey and feed it to the bird with an eyedropper.

Joey died with a smile on his beak and was buried, with full honors, in a shoebox in our backyard.

Or while in college at the University of Illinois, when I was employed by my landlady to care for the lawns of three properties that she owned. While cutting the grass at one location, I came upon a robin that had lodged one of its feet in between two slats of a closely spaced picket fence. In its frantic effort to free itself, it had broken the leg in half and was flapping its wings violently, back and forth, leaving a semicircle of blood on the fence. I carefully freed the bird, gently wrapped it in a clean towel, and drove fifteen miles to the university's veterinary hospital to save its life, where the vet student looked at me as if to say, "What do you want us to do with it?" but said, "We'll see what we can do." This probably meant they would put it out of its misery, but that was their karma now. I did my part and felt good about it.

Suffice it to say, I believe that all animals deserve as much respect and dignity in this universe as we humans do.

According to the National Parkinson Foundation, pet therapy with "lap" animals, especially dogs and cats, can provide great satisfaction in the lives of their human companions. Studies have shown that having animals in the home improves both mental and emotional health of their owners, not to mention creating ample opportunities for movement and exercise. Pet therapy can lower the blood pressure and heart rate of their owners; improve mobility and flexibility; and satisfy the human need for touch and nurturing.

Murphy is our Golden Retriever. Since a very young age, Murphy has suffered from epilepsy. A typical epileptic event starts with him falling quickly to the ground as his legs curl tightly beneath his body. Then he slowly begins to convulse. His mouth is clenched tight, as are most of the muscles in his body. If we are fortunate enough to be there with him when he has a seizure, we will lie by his side and gently pet him, reassuring him that we are there. Usually, after about ten to fifteen minutes, the seizure ends and, after some rest, he returns to his legs. Murphy has about two or three of these events per month.

He is on a daily regimen of Phenobarbital, Dasquin and Colby Jack. The Phenobarbital is an anticonvulsant to help control his seizures; the Dasquin is a joint supplement to aid his hips and legs; and the Colby Jack is a cheese. That's the only way he'll take his pills.

In addition to his epilepsy, Murphy has had two ACL surgeries, one on each of his hind legs, about one year apart. The culprit was, most likely, the amorous play between Murphy and our neighbor's Bernese mountain dog, Kensington.

At the age of ten, poor Murphy is being ravaged by severe arthritis in his hips. Rising from his bed is a struggle, not to mention climbing or descending stairs. But being a retriever, he instinctually wants to bring you something every time you come into the house, so he still manages it—he just does it much slower.

They say owners often resemble their dogs. Murphy and I definitely have some unique similarities.

What amazes me most about Murphy is that, with all he has dealt with—the seizures and surgeries he has endured, and all the difficulty and discomfort he now faces with arthritis—he continues to wag his tail. He still manages to produce a dog's version of a human smile.

Murphy has great attitude and he gives me strength.

A secondary symptom of Parkinson's disease that can develop is the loss of facial expression due to rigidity of facial muscles, called hypomimia. It is often described as an expressionless mask on the individual's face, as if they haven't any ability to show emotion.

With hypomimia comes the inability to smile.

It is important to note that no one individual develops all the possible symptoms of Parkinson's disease The nature of PD, as well as the rate of progression, varies greatly from one individual to another.

In all honesty, the potential of losing my ability to smile is my greatest concern with my Parkinson's disease, because my smile is who I am. My smile is a mirror I hold up to all those people that are in my life—it allows me the opportunity to let them see themselves and the joy they bring, as well as how rich they make me feel. My smile is my way of saying thank you.

From my earliest days in grade school, I was the class clown. My report cards, and more specifically the *comments* on them from the teachers, could attest to that. I simply loved sharing my happiness with life, even to the point that it got me in trouble.

I choose to make fun of Parkinson's disease, not because I lack respect for what it does to people, but because I choose to take something unpleasant and find some humor in it. If I'm going to live with it, I might as well find the fun in it. I smile because that's what my grandfather—the man I never had the opportunity to meet—would have done. The man who, I was always told, was smiling. The man who was smiling in every picture I ever saw of him. And the man who my masseuse Staci saw smiling when he visited her in a vision.

My concern over losing my smile is so great, that I have made it a part of my exercise routine.

Every morning between 5:30 and 6 a.m., I make my way downstairs to my treadmill and begin my walk that lasts anywhere from forty-five minutes to an hour. While walking, I use this important time to meditate, to rejuvenate, to focus my energies on good health, and to set the tone for the day's success. I make a conscious effort to bring everything to bear toward beating back Parkinson's. With positive thoughts and energy, as well as the help of talented doctors, and effort on my part, I truly believe I can have a positive relationship with Parkinson's.

After I'm well into my workout, Murphy makes his way slowly down the stairs and lies by the door of the room. He flashes me his smile with a wag of his tail. That's my cue to add one more element to my workout routine.

While walking on the treadmill, I actually do some facial exercises like an opera singer warming up. Exaggerating the muscles of my face, I form two sounds with my mouth, first a "wee" followed by an "ooh", and then back and forth. The wee forms the smile and the ooh relaxes the face. I do twenty sets of ten while Murphy encourages me with his wagging tail.

I believe Murphy has the ability to feel the same spiritual connection with me that I feel with him. He understands my smile as the happiness he brings to me, like the wag of his tail tells me how much I mean to him.

Keep smiling.

CHAPTER 24

HAPPY NEW DAY

"There are only two days in the year that nothing can be done. One is called Yesterday and the other is called Tomorrow. So Today is the right day to Love, Believe, Do and mostly, Live." ~Dalai Lama

As I got ready to say goodbye to 2013 and ring in the New Year, I had been thinking about how we look at the past and how we look at the future—and ultimately, how our perspectives are changed by life's events.

I am sure quite a few individuals were anxious to say goodbye to 2013 because it may have brought them emotional hardship, perhaps the passing of a loved one or a difficult year financially.

Maybe they're Cubs fans.

At the same time, there are the countless others that saw the past year as a fantastic one. Maybe they celebrated a wedding or a birth, or received a promotion.

Again, it simply is a matter of personal experience and perception.

I was given my Parkinson's diagnosis in 2012. On July 11th of that year, I didn't have Parkinson's disease—at least, not by a confirming diagnosis—but on the following day, July 12th, I did. For all intents and purposes, I truly didn't feel any different physically from one day to the next.

Emotionally, it's another story. As mentioned earlier, receiving my diagnosis actually came as a huge relief for me. Finally having an answer to my physical problems was actually empowering. It gave me something to understand, something to accept and something to manage.

But physically? From one day to the next—no worse, no better; just, the same.

It was the information that had changed for me, and with that new knowledge, I immediately had a choice as to what I would make of the experience—the experience *that is*, the experience *that will be*, Parkinson's.

An *Event*. An *Experience*. A *Choice*.

That's pretty much what life is, over and over and over again.

Within each moment of each day of our lives, we have *events* that occur; outside stimuli that affect us personally. It can come in the form of a perceived, indirect event like watching the news: seeing that the market was up or down, or that a hurricane had devastated a third world country. Or perhaps, by observing someone on the street giving money to a homeless person. It can be a personal event, like losing your job, winning the lottery, going on a blind date or receiving a diagnosis of cancer. The number of unperceived events that occur to each of us every day is staggering. There are more than we could possibly process. But it's the selective events that we *do* perceive, and the affect each one has on us, that shape and mold our lives into the individual we ultimately become.

Each person has the power to decide what an *experience* will be to them. It can be positive and therefore one you'd like to repeat, or it can be a negative one you'd rather avoid repeating. Neither is right or wrong, simply an experience—a learning process and step towards spiritual growth.

The same event can provide entirely unique experiences for different people. Take, for example, observing someone on the street giving money to a homeless person. One individual might be inspired to pay it forward, and make a donation for someone in need, or get involved with a homeless shelter. Another person, however, might think that the person who gave the money is only contributing to this panhandler's alcohol or drug addiction. Yet another individual might turn a blind eye to the scene entirely. None are right or wrong; they are simply individual and personal experiences.

That ultimately brings us to the third element, which is *choice*. From every event in our lives and the experiences we have as a result of them, we have a choice. We have a choice as to how the events and our experience with them will define our actions?

Children starving in a third world country (or even right here in the United States) bring about an experience for most of sadness and disgust. Some actually go as far as to question how God could allow this to happen. Yet it is *our* choice to let the experience repeat itself or to put an end to it. There is enough food in the world to feed everyone if we just made the choice to do so.

The personal choice of what we do with our experiences is the most powerful "God-given" gift we have. The driving force behind my own choices comes back to my intuition—my heart, my gut and my mind. If I listen to my intuition when I make my choices and if I make them from a place of love, then I can't go wrong.

Yes, I have Parkinson's. But I'm still the same person, with the same heart, the same smile and the same love of life. I still have to wear glasses, and I am still a Cubs fan. Things aren't perfect in my life, but they sure are good. And every day when I get on my treadmill, I give thanks for that day, because the event for the day is the fact that I am here. The experience is life and to me it is wonderful. My choice is to keep repeating it.

Happy New Day.

CHAPTER 25

INFINITE POSSIBILITIES

"There once was an old man who took long walks on the beach every morning. One day he saw a young man dancing in the distance. As he got closer, he realized he wasn't dancing at all, but reaching down and throwing small crabs into the sea. "Young man, what are you doing?" he asked. "Throwing crabs back into the sea" the young man replied, "they'll die if I don't help them." The old man looked down at the hundreds of small crabs scattered on the beach for miles. "But there must be millions of them," the old man told him, aghast. "You can't possibly make a difference." The young man bent down, picked up another crab and threw it into the ocean. "It made a difference to that one.""

~Anonymous

As I walked on my treadmill on this first morning of the New Year, I was thinking a lot about potential—specifically, the potential for 2014. Not only about what it holds for me, but the possibilities it holds for my family and my friends who I know faced hardship in 2013. I hope and prayed that 2014 would bring positive change to all the people I love. The more I thought about it, a new year does indeed hold the potential for positive change for everyone.

It's very appropriate that our symbol for the New Year is a baby. A baby represents a new beginning. A baby has limitless potential from that very first second it comes into this world. Stop and think about this. At the moment of birth, every infant born has the same infinite potential to learn ANY language in the entire universe. The brain is a pure sponge capable of soaking up whatever it is exposed to, ready to learn, accept and experience without judgment, because it knew nothing else to judge against. It has pure, limitless possibility.

The environment in which we are each raised puts that first limit on our potential. We learn the language we are exposed to. But the universe doesn't just hold potential for language, it holds the potential for every piece of knowledge in the same way. It's all out there, and we all have the potential to soak it up. However, we learn what we are presented with and do what we are conditioned to do, and if that's all we ever strive for, it's all we will gain. Actively pushing past those limits to reach our potential is the hardest part.

At the stroke of midnight on December 31st, January 1st enters the world like a newborn baby, with limitless potential as well. So do each of us. As the new year enters, we may know nothing about what it holds for us, but it's full of potential, so it's up to us to not put any limitations upon it.

Our goal for the new year should be to make a change—a change in our thinking, in ourselves and in our world. Insist on positive results. Make a difference—in your life or another's.

I choose to believe that the potential for everything is out there. The cure for Parkinson's is out in the universe. It's there. We just haven't found it yet. The potential cure for everything is. We just need to keep searching, always willing to make changes in how we look and where we look.

The potential to make positive change in our selves exists in the universe, too. It requires perseverance and a willingness to keep looking in different places. Everything we do does make a difference in our lives and the lives of others.

Like the story of the young man throwing crabs back into the sea, will you be more like the old man with a narrow view of the big picture; or will you be like the young man who sees potential in the smaller things you can do to make a difference along the way? We're all going to have roadblocks and failures along the path of life. We may never get all the crabs back in the sea. But we can each make a difference with each little change we make.

My father-in-law who passed away this past fall had a wonderful saying that he used to equate to saving money: "Add a little to a little and do it often, and in time you'll have great things." I like that saying because to me it also means, "Make small, positive changes in your life and the lives of others and do them often, and in time you'll have changed the world."

I think my father-in-law must have been that young man on the beach.

Here's to the potential of a new year.

Chapter 26
Constant Patience

When I first started writing *Tremors in the Universe*, the pages came quickly and easily, but sometimes you just get a blockage that keeps you from putting something down. No matter how hard you try to be productive, you just end up sitting there with nothing to show for your time and effort. You have the paper ready but...

Butt nothing.

Trust me. It's incredibly frustrating. Before Parkinson's I never had this problem. When I sat with my thoughts, well, ideas just flowed.

Then finally it occurred to me, I could write about the problem itself. My only concern is, it's such a sensitive subject, that some people might be offended and make a bigger stink of it than it really is, which could easily wipe away all the good work I've tried to accomplish.

But the subject is most definitely a problem that affects Parkinson's patients, 42% of them at last report. The Michael J. Fox Foundation even has a clinical trial devoted to research to try and lead to some relief for PD patients who suffer from this symptom.

The purpose of my writing has always been more than just working out my own feelings related to Parkinson's and spirituality. I've hoped that, in some small way, it might help others as well.

So, with that in mind...I hesitantly push ahead.

The title of this chapter pretty much sums it up. This is an innuendo-filled (or maybe I should say, in-your-end-oh!-filled), light-hearted, yet serious look at a secondary Parkinson's disease symptom that truly does impact countless patients. That's right, folks. Pull up a stool and get ready for the warm, hard facts about the number two cause of distress for PD patients, and that is...constipation.

There. I said it.

It's definitely something I wouldn't wish on my worst enema and quite frankly it isn't very easy to talk about—but I'd be lax if I didn't try.

So what is our hang up with talking about constipation? Well, first of all it's the name itself: constipation. It's one of those words that you naturally whisper when you say it, like it's something to be ashamed of. Diarrhea is the loose-lipped cousin of constipation and we whisper that name, too. While Pepto-Bismol did a pretty good job of bringing diarrhea out of the water closet, I think I'm just the guy to get people to loosen up about constipation.

Perhaps for the purposes of our dialogue, we should push hard for a new name that we can use without hesitation.

In 479 BC, the ancient Chinese philosopher, Confucius, referred to it as HungChow, but I find I can relate more to the Latin roots of the word constipation, which translates to "constant patience."

I knew Parkinson's was characterized as a movement disorder, but gee—really?

As I said earlier, constant patience affects 42% of Parkinson's patients as compared with just 7% of the general population. It is often prevalent in early stages of PD, yet most patients suffer in silence due to the delicate nature of discussing the symptoms with their doctor. Left untreated however, recurrent constant patience can lead to impaction of the colon, ultimately requiring hospitalization.

According to the Parkinson's Disease Foundation (PDF), constant patience in Parkinson's patients is due to slowed travel of material through the colon, which can be a result of PD medications or the neurological effects of PD itself. The first step in treating this decreased colonic motility is by increasing fluid and fiber intake. According to the PDF, current recommendations suggest that daily fiber intake should be in the range of 20 to 35 grams, but the average American only consumes around 14 grams. Fiber intake can be increased through dietary measures, by eating more grains and cereals; legumes and beans; and fruits and vegetables—or by taking fiber supplements.

One effective remedy I've discovered is what I like to call my morning caca-tail or, for a *really* fun bar name, the "Porcelain Wallbanger."

Porcelain Wallbanger

- 2 cups prune juice
- 2 cups apple sauce
- 6 tbsp. wheat germ

Mix all ingredients together in a martini shaker. Take one shotglass-sized serving (approximately 1 to 2 tablespoons) each morning at first to see your system's response.

The PDF says that if increasing fiber and fluid intake is not adequately effective, the next step can be to add a stool softener. If the problem still persists, the doctor may suggest initiation of an agent that draws fluid into the colon, such as Lactulose. If that does not help with the problem, daily doses of a colon-cleansing agent such as MiraLAX® may be employed. And if all else fails, it may be necessary to resort to enemas, but only under the supervision of a physician.

The theme for the National Parkinson Foundation's Moving Day Chicago walk was "Just Keep Moving", which focused on the importance of exercise for maintaining good muscle health, increasing flexibility and physical mobility. Well, exercise is also shown to hold additional positive benefits in keeping PD patients "moving" even when they're sitting down. Want to "keep moving"? Then keep moving!

In yet another effort to get to the bottom of the problem, the Michael J. Fox Foundation enrolled patients in a clinical trial at Michigan State University in East Lansing, Michigan. You can visit the MJF Foundation online for a complete list of trials at www.foxtrialfinder.michaeljfox.org.

No matter how you choose to approach the problem of constant patience (although I highly recommend from the front), it's good to know there are solutions available. Remember, it's always extremely important to discuss *any* symptoms with your doctor.

For those of you that I haven't managed to offend, I'd like you to join me in raising a glass of Porcelain Wallbanger and toast the good health of all Parkinson's patients.

Bottoms up!

Chapter 27

Trust

Never hide who you are or be afraid to share your beliefs out of fear of someone having a problem with them. Stand tall and have faith in what you believe, and don't let others tell you you're wrong. Also, don't try to convince others that *they're* wrong. Truths are relative, not absolute. Tolerance is divine.

Spiritual by definition is something that is not tangible in nature. It is immaterial, not of solid mass. Intuitively, I'm of the personal belief that each of us, spiritually, is energy, and that our spiritual essence is a part of the larger energy of the universe—an energy we cannot see, but which most of us feel in our hearts.

Our physical body, I'm sure all of us can agree, has a very measurable mass.

Yet Einstein's theory of relativity, $E=mc^2$, means that mass and energy are basically two forms of the same thing. Energy is matter that's been liberated or released, and matter or mass is energy waiting to happen.

According to Pam Groot's New York Times bestseller, *E-squared*, the average human contains no less than 7 times 10 to the 18th power joules of potential energy. If you were capable of liberating that energy, you could use it to explode yourself with the force of thirty very large hydrogen bombs. That's a lot of energy. And that would make a huge mess of you, so please don't do that.

So by my theory (and I am no Einstein), combining all of that information, each of us as human beings have at our core or our essence, spiritual energy—a *lot* of spiritual energy. And the combination of all the energy there is in the universe, from humans and other living things, ultimately would bring us to the realization of God—or pure life energy, or whatever you want to call it. The only thing preventing that from occurring is that the majority of all of that energy remains only *potential*. We don't use it. We concentrate on the material, the physical, the things and the events we can see.

For myself, personally, I plan on changing that. My goal is to tap into all the potential spiritual energy I have, to make positive changes for myself. Managing my Parkinson's disease is one area I know that will benefit.

To me, spiritual enlightenment occurs when we manage to bring to a state of consciousness what we already know subconsciously. It's comprehending and then putting into practice what we feel intuitively. It's an acceptance that we are all part of a bigger energy that binds us together, so while our individual choices profoundly affect our own experiences, they also affect the lives and spiritual growth of those around us. With each connection we make in our lives, a gift is given and a gift is received, and through our own spiritual convictions we hold gifts for ourselves as well.

For spiritual enlightenment to take place, two things must happen. First, we have to be aware of and able to listen to our intuition. Second, we have to be able to consciously accept what we hear and what we feel as our spiritual truth. We must trust our intuition in order to trust our *self*.

"Spirituality lies not in the power to heal others, to perform miracles, or to astound the world with our wisdom, but in the ability to endure, with right attitude, whatever crosses we have to face in our daily lives, and thus to rise above them."
~ Sri Daya Mata Ji

From the very first moment of my diagnosis, I have felt in my gut that I would be fine with my relationship with Parkinson's disease. Yet, in all honesty, I didn't know why or what that even meant. What does "fine" mean? Was the sense of contentment I felt coming from a conviction that I would never experience any drastic, life-altering effects of Parkinson's disease? Or that I could simply handle whatever PD gave me, regardless of severity?

What I came to realize, was that it really wasn't consciously coming from one or the other. It was coming from my intuition. From that very first moment, I have continued to trust that feeling—that inner voice.

Not only did that trust sustain me in the beginning, but it has given rise to even greater empowerment since then.

My trust has transposed to my belief system and the idea behind the Law of Attraction. That like attracts like. That my having positive thoughts about my health and my relationship with Parkinson's, will bring about positive results. I trust that to be true because I feel it in my gut and believe it with all my heart. At the very least, the positivity I presently feel about Parkinson's is proof enough for me to continue with that train of thought.

I would not begin to say I am doing this alone, nor do I want to do this alone. I welcome the knowledge and the gifts that my doctors hold for me, and I welcome the support and love that I receive from family and friends. I see them all as positive affirmations returning to me from my own positive thoughts.

By maintaining this attitude, I am bringing into my conscious mind what I have always felt intuitively, in my subconscious. Like ripples on a pond, the effects keep growing. Ripples become waves, and waves become tsunamis. And it all began simply with my willingness, my intention and my trust.

It is my sincere belief there is a reason behind everything that happens— negative experiences as well as positive. It's easy to make that determination when we've made it through the fire, but more difficult to keep in mind when a challenging event is upon us. That is truly when we need to rely on intuition and our trust in our own spirit.

Ego says: "Once everything falls into place, I will find peace;." Whereas Spirit says: "Find peace and everything will fall into place."
~Anonymous

I've definitely found my peace with Parkinson's and I do trust everything will fall into place. And that gives me comfort.

CHAPTER 28

CAREGIVER VS. SCAREGIVER

"We need people in our lives with whom we can be as open as possible. To have real conversations with people may seem like such a simple, obvious suggestion, but it involves courage and risk." ~Thomas Moore

As you can probably tell by now, I am a very shy individual who has a difficult time opening up and talking to people. Why, the mere idea of sharing my personal views on my spirituality and exposing my experiences with Parkinson's makes me incredibly uncomfortable.

Thankfully, my twelve years of speaking in public school (which usually landed me alone with my desk in the hall, the Dean's office or detention), along with two years of Speech Communications at the University of Illinois, four years of design school presentations for project critique, combined with twenty-five years of business presentations, have taken some of the edge away.

All kidding aside, truly opening up to people with honest dialogue, like the quotation above suggests, *does* involve courage and risk.

When I first received my diagnosis, I researched on the internet as most people do. While I found plenty of websites outlining the specifics of Parkinson's— from foundations and support groups to medical reference sites—I found very little that offered deeply personal accounts of living with this disease. Not many writers seemed to be willing to take the risk. So when I made the decision to write, in addition to it being informative to my children and therapeutic to myself, I vowed to create open and honest dialogue for the benefit of other Parkinson's patients. If that meant discussing very personal aspects of the disease in my day-to-day life, then so be it. I wanted to write with a sincere and credible voice. If I was going to "talk", I was going to speak loudly.

For a vast majority of Parkinson's patients, public speaking can truly be a significant problem. According to The National Center for Voice and Speech, researchers estimate that eighty-nine percent of people with Parkinson's disease have speech and voice disorders.

Dysarthria is one of the secondary symptoms experienced by some Parkinson's patients, and is characterized by low voice volume or muffled speech, among other symptoms.

Prior to starting the regimen of medications I am presently on, this used to be a common occurrence for me. As each day progressed, my voice would become weaker and weaker and mildly hoarse (sexy on a woman, not so much on a guy). It was a serious concern for me because the success of my business relied on verbal presentations and the ability to sell my ideas through detailed description.

The importance of clear communication for Parkinson's patients goes beyond the obvious every day need for clearly spoken words. It needs to take place at a personal level within their relationships—with doctors, friends and family. It requires candid discussions of not only their symptoms, but their thoughts and feelings as well. Parkinson's is an extremely individual experience, so the only true way for others to understand one's personal journey with it is by showing the courage to have this open dialogue.

The same holds true for relationships in general. A quote from Khalil Gibran sums up the importance of quality communication rather well: "Between what is said and not meant, and what is meant and not said, most of love is lost."

Keep in mind quality dialogue is a two way street.

As important as it is for people with Parkinson's to maintain their voice and share their feelings, it is equally important that they maintain their ability to hear, to listen and to allow others to open up to them as well. They should keep in mind that they are not the only one who is affected by Parkinson's. Their loved ones are affected as well.

That's where I made a mistake.

As the popularity of my online blog began to grow, I began receiving emails from readers who enjoyed reading it. They sent well wishes and hoped that I would continue with my positive attitude. In fact, I received a lot of wonderful feedback from a variety people—except from one person in particular: my wife.

What I had neglected to do was ask her how *she* was doing with my Parkinson's diagnosis. Instead, I simply assumed she had taken on the same positive attitude I had, and that she also believed everything was going to be just fine. As I eventually discovered, that was not how she saw it or felt about it at all; on the contrary. My wife was very scared of my having Parkinson's, though she never wanted to say anything for fear that she might diminish my positive attitude. While I had come to the conclusion that she had no interest in my writing, the truth eventually surfaced that she was basically too frightened to read what I was writing about.

Whether it is your partner, a family member, a friend or a caregiver, each person deserves the same attention to feelings and emotional well being as we do as Parkinson's patients.

Take the risk. Speak up. And don't forget to listen.

CHAPTER 29

PICKUP OR DELIVERY?

"Millions of people never analyze themselves. Mentally they become mechanical products of the factory of their environment, preoccupied with breakfast, lunch, and dinner, working and sleeping, and going here and there to be entertained. They don't know what they are seeking or why, nor do they ever come to understand why they never realize complete happiness and lasting satisfaction. By evading self-analysis, people go on being robots, conditioned by their environment. True self-analysis is the greatest art of progress." ~Spiritual Evolution

Flying, Pizza, Art, Vodka, Parkinson's and Blogging.

That list of words that sum up my Twitter profile reminds me of the cognitive testing at my Parkinson's PPMI clinical trial appointments. (Remember the test where Christina would give me a list of ten words, then ask me later in the session to recall as many as I could?)

However, these six words are ones I came up with on my own to best sum up what I am passionate about in life.

Talk about self-analysis.

It reads more like I'm some kind of laid back, head-in-the-clouds, artsy type who spends his time eating pizza, drinking vodka and writing about Parkinson's.

Wow. I really need to start getting out more.

With the exception of the vodka, the interesting thing about that list is, they all have a strong relationship to each other in creating the map of my life—a map that, surprisingly enough, always starts out on one planned course, just to have the route altered, requiring a new approach to reach my destination. But like my experience with Parkinson's, having flexibility and a willingness to choose another direction can make all the difference in the world.

Aviation.

I pursued two different degrees in college—not at the same time, mind you. No, I simply enjoyed college life, spending eight years on a campus and managing to graduate without a medical degree, a PhD or a Masters. What I did earn however, were various pilot ratings, a Bachelors of Fine Arts degree in Graphic Design, and an appreciation for great pizza.

Flying had become my passion just a few short years before heading off to college. My best friend in high school's father had his pilot's license, and one weekend Scott and his dad took me along for a flight. In all honesty, it was the first time I had ever even been in an airplane. I grew up in a family of very modest means, so family vacations always meant driving within the States. So this flight was amazing—something about it just struck a chord with me. That moment that the tires left the runway and the plane transformed into metal floating on air, was pure magic. I was hooked.

I actually became so obsessed with flying, that after picking up Scott in the morning for high school, we'd sometimes call his mom from a pay phone, asking her to inform the school we'd be late due to a flat tire. Then we would drive to Chicago's O'Hare airport to watch the planes come in. Once in awhile we'd approach a pilot and ask him if we could buy him lunch, just to have the opportunity to talk about flying.

I started taking flight lessons at the age of sixteen, so by the time of my high school graduation, I was presented with my first opportunity to choose a path regarding where my future would take me.

I had all of the State Representatives endorsements needed, and met all the requirements to attend the United States Air Force Academy; or I could choose to utilize a small scholarship I had received for pursuing a career in aviation at Southern Illinois University. The choice was mine. How did I want to get from point A to point B?

I wouldn't decide on the Air Force Academy for two very distinct reasons. First, there was no guarantee I would be accepted into flight school after completing my basic education at the Academy; and second, I couldn't pull the trigger. I mean just that. I wouldn't have been able to pull the trigger. The thought of going to war during that time presented a scenario I had long known I wasn't cut out for. I simply was not the kind of soldier the Air Force would want, nor should I be taking away an opportunity from someone who was.

So...Southern Illinois University–Carbondale, here I come.

And one year later?

Illinois and University of Illinois–Champaign-Urbana, here I come.

Apparently my path in life was going to take a bit of a detour, from point A to point B, to point C.

Although Carbondale was a fantastic school, I made the switch to the U of I because I felt it had a better reputation. Maybe I was taking what my mom always said and restating it my way: "Bob has *Champaign* taste on a beer budget."

The next two-and-a-half years of flight school went by quickly and I soon saw graduation looming on the horizon, the next leg of my journey rapidly approaching. I started to inquire with my faculty about the best route toward obtaining a corporate flying position—you know, so I could be flying rock bands around the country from gig to gig.

Take out the life map again. I had two options.

"You can enlist in the military for another four years to get your jet time for free; or you can enroll at Embry-Riddle Aeronautical University in Florida and pay $10,000 for your jet time there," I was informed.

The military question had been answered long ago, so that wasn't an option. Unfortunately, after three-and-a-half years of college, I truly was on a beer budget—very, very cheap beer.

Pizza.

Disillusioned, I took the next year off from college to try to determine my new path in life. I took a job as an assistant manager of a pizza restaurant on campus. Actually, not *a* pizza restaurant; it was, and is, *the* pizza restaurant— Papa Del's Pizza, by far the best thin and deep-dish pizza there is. Trust me. I'm from Chicago. I know pizza, and I have tasted quite a few. If you think you know of a better pizza, you're wrong. But if you insist that I am wrong, then please send me a full-size pie and I will be happy to give it my honest consideration.

The owner of Papa Del's, "Pops", really had only hired me for one reason: because I was a pilot.

Pops was a successful businessman (not hard when you have the best pizza in the world), and owned a number of restaurants on Big Ten college campuses. He wasn't a very trusting man, and always thought his employees were out to take his money. Therefore, he saw the hiring of an assistant manager/pilot as an opportunity to make unannounced "fly-in" inspections of his other operations. He was out to catch them pocketing his dough, so to speak.

Our first flight was to Purdue in West Lafayette, Indiana, in the month of February. The day was sunny and the air was crisp. The general manager Bob, Pops and myself would make the trip together.

The flight to Indiana was uneventful. Bob sat next to me with a pair of binoculars and Pops sat directly behind me. The flight in our rented, four-seater Beechcraft took a little over an hour. On the ground, Pops and Bob went into town for their stealth inspection, while I remained at the airport where I could periodically check in with flight services for weather updates.

At the time, I was ten hours of instruction time short of my IFR (instrument flight rule) rating, which would license me to fly in conditions where there was no visibility. Until that rating is achieved, a pilot is VFR (visual flight rule) rated and is only licensed to fly using visual cues—basically, when it's clear outside.

A little over two hours had gone by when one of my check-ins with flight services yielded the information a VFR pilot does not want to hear: there was a rapidly moving snowstorm coming in from the west that was presently hitting Peoria, Illinois, about an hour or so from Champaign. The storm was reportedly reducing visibility down to a eighth of a mile. I would have just enough time to beat the storm back if we could leave immediately.

I called Pops, and after explaining the situation and the urgent need for his return, I proceeded to get our plane refueled and did my pre-flight walk around. As soon as they returned I would be ready to depart.

The time it took Pops and Bob to get back to the airport would prove to be a very crucial twenty minutes. I was about to face another life or death situation, an event that would not only test my convictions and focus, but would also serve to prepare me for dealing with my future diagnosis of Parkinson's.

Luckily I had rented a four-seater. We had an extra seat for my guardian angel.

I taxied our Beechcraft onto the runway and came to a complete stop. Alignment was perfect, nose wheel on the centerline. I had full brakes applied and I was running through the final pre-flight checklist. *Flaps?* Check. *Fuel gauge?* Check. *Altimeter?* Check. *Rudder and ailerons?* Check. We were ready to go.

The moment of take off was always the most anxious time for me, because that's when the plane's flight stability is most vulnerable. If a pilot stalls an airplane on takeoff or loses an engine, he's in trouble really quick. If you lose the engine at ten thousand feet, you can actually glide the plane down if need be, but lose it at two hundred fifty feet or, worse yet, stall the plane, and there really isn't enough time to recover.

Today as I sat in the cockpit looking down the runway, my right hand on the throttle, my thoughts were not on the takeoff, but already a good hour ahead in time, imagining what I would be flying into. A snowstorm was rapidly approaching Champaign, Illinois, our final destination.

I almost felt hesitancy in my hand as I went to push the throttle, but with a little effort it slid forward and the engine roared to life. I released the brakes and the airplane began its roll out. At this point during the takeoff, a pilot is basically driving the airplane with his feet, the left and right pedals turning the nose wheel to keep it aligned with the runway. The steering wheel controls the ailerons for lifting the plane off the ground, once critical speed for maintaining flight has been reached.

With a firm pull back on the wheel, we were floating on air. As we continued our climb, there was no sweeter sound than the roar of the engine.

"November Alpha five four eight, turn to a heading of two seven zero and continue to twenty-five hundred," air traffic control announced over the radio. I turned the airplane from north to west and I could suddenly see on the horizon just what we were going to be flying into. The engine of the airplane was roaring strong, but my heart had just stalled and was sinking rapidly into my stomach.

On the distant horizon was a dark gray ceiling of clouds. Just beneath it, as if someone were lifting up a veil, was the golden color of the late winter sky. As I looked from left to right, the gray ceiling above that traversed the gold below suddenly dove to the ground as if the gray were being sucked to the earth. Where the gray met terra firma, it continued for a while to the right before lifting skyward again.

I turned to Bob and asked him if he had his binoculars handy. "Look at the horizon. Do you see that area of clouds that reaches down to the ground out in the distance? That's where we are heading. That's in line with Champaign."

He brought the binoculars to his eyes, studied the horizon for a while, and then slowly brought them back to his lap without saying a word.

The next forty-five minutes of the flight were filled with conversation between Bob and Pops as they reviewed their recent blitzkrieg of the West Lafayette Papa Del's restaurant, while I was routinely passed from one flight control center to another along our route. Each flight control center monitors the planes in their area until you reach their outer boundary and then they pass you off to the next region with a new radio setting and a sign off of, "Have a good day."

All the while, I was keeping a vigilant eye on the rapidly approaching gray wall in the distance.

Flying inside clouds without any solid visual reference outside of the plane can wreak havoc with a pilot's sense of balance and equilibrium, forcing even the best-trained pilot to question everything their brain is telling them. Even though from a distance the clouds may look gray, fly inside one and the cockpit becomes a bright white that creates the illusion of flying in a glass of milk. There is simply no discerning up from down using your eyes only.

Today, however, the clouds we were flying into weren't going to create the illusion of milk—it was going to be more like ice cream.

Just prior to entering the Champaign flight control's airspace for the final leg of our flight, the snowflakes started to come down. What began as light flurries that might have looked festive in a holiday snow globe, quickly picked up momentum. Within a matter of minutes, my three-mile visibility was reduced to a half-mile, then to a quarter. This definitely was not looking good.

"Champaign Center, this is November Alpha five four eight at four thousand five hundred. VFR," I radioed to make contact now with our new host.

"Roger November Alpha five four eight, maintain two seven zero and descend to four thousand. Did I hear you correctly as VFR?" Center responded back.

"Affirmative," I verified.

The series of events that followed would become a metaphor for my future diagnosis of Parkinson's and my subsequent determination to persevere. In both instances, my mettle would be tested. I would discover that it was within my character to find a different approach—a different way of seeing things—when my vision was being obscured and I very easily could have given up on my journey.

"November Alpha five four eight, this is Champaign Center. VFR clearance is denied. Present airport visibility is less than an eighth of a mile with heavy snow."

"Champaign Center this is November Alpha five four eight requesting special VFR," which I knew was like an objection in a court of law. I was arguing one more time for my right to land if I could manage to make visual contact with the runway myself—sort of like saying, "Come on, just give me a shot."

"Negative November Alpha five four eight."

To eliminate a majority of the airport jargon, suffice it to say that what transpired next was to basically ask Champaign control what my options were. I was fifteen miles out from the airport and desperately wanted to get this plane, my passengers and myself safely on the ground. Champaign control responded that I had two options available to me. One, I could turn the plane around and return to West Lafayette; or two, they could vector me (give me a compass heading) over an uncontrolled airport, and if I could manage to see the runway myself, I was free to land there (sort of their way of wiping their hands of me).

Decision time. I looked at the fuel gauge and determined there was enough for the return flight. Out the front windshield of the plane, I could only see a kaleidoscope of snowflakes. A quick glance out the side window and directly downward offered me a view of the ground going by.

"Champaign Center, this is November Alpha five four eight requesting special VFR vectoring."

I was provided a compass heading to turn to and was told that, if I could make visual contact with the uncontrolled airport's runway, they would then release me to the frequency of that airport and I would be on my own. After about ten minutes on my new heading, Champaign informed me that the runway should be coming up directly ahead. I still had no forward visibility beyond an eighth of a mile, so I was still looking out the side window and downward. As I watched the snow-covered ground going by, I suddenly saw the runway pass by below.

"Champaign Center, November Alpha five four eight has visual contact."

"November Alpha five four eight, switch frequency to 118.50. Good day. And good luck."

Hmmmm. I'd never heard that one before.

I knew that, based on the wind direction and the direction of the runway I had just flown over, that I needed to quickly make a left turn to enter into the downwind leg of my landing pattern. At my altitude, if I took that leg of the rectangle out a good mile, then I could turn my base leg and follow that for a minute before turning in for my final approach—which was all well and good, but I never had tried this before with such limited forward visibility. Landing procedures are busy enough under normal circumstances, let alone during a February snowstorm.

I lowered flaps to reduce my airspeed, because with the risk of a slick runway it was going to be best to come in extremely slow. If the plane started to slide on the runway, I could just cut the engine and coast to a stop.

Turning base leg. Check to make sure everyone's buckled in.

"All tray tables are stowed and seats are in an upright position? Does anyone need to use the bathroom?" I jokingly asked Pops and Bob with a smile. No one was smiling back.

Turning final.

Ok, it's got to be straight ahead here, I kept saying to myself. Altitude is five hundred feet. Engine speed is good. I have one hand on the wheel, both feet working the rudder and one hand on the throttle in case I need to do a go-around.

To stay "current" in flight school (which means to keep your pilot's license active), you have to do three "touch-and-go's" every ninety days. Touch-and-go's mean going through the complete landing procedure all the way through touch down: then, as the plane is rolling, giving it full throttle and taking off immediately without stopping the airplane. It's a great preparation for just a scenario like this.

At an altitude of three hundred feet, I made visual contact with the runway about an eighth of a mile ahead. Unfortunately, it's well off to the right by about one hundred to two hundred yards. An abrupt adjustment on the plane's course, in an attempt to make the runway, could result in disaster. So I quickly gunned the engine with full throttle, pulled back on the wheel and began climbing out again. I entered the crosswind leg of my landing pattern before turning downwind and starting the whole procedure over again.

I swear that, by all my calculations, I'd repeated everything I had done the first time. Only on this second approach, the runway was a good one hundred to two hundred yards off again—in the opposite direction.

Full throttle. Pull back on the wheel. We're going around again.

During that third attempt, something wonderful happened to me. Rather than giving in to exasperation and letting desperation set in, a sense of calm and clarity came over me, giving me a creative way to gain control over my situation. Intuition told me that everything was going to be ok. I just needed to look at things differently. Ironically, I needed to change my approach.

With no traffic in the area due to the heavy snow, I decided to divert from the customary rectangular landing pattern that took me a good half-mile to the side, parallel to the runway. Instead, I chose to fly straight forward along the runway as I climbed back out before doing a quick, hard one-eighty degree turn that brought me directly over the runway again, facing the opposite direction of my normal final approach.

Flying over the runway and proceeding farther out, I kept my eyes out the side window, watching the ground as the runway slowly disappeared behind me.

Then I noticed: A tree. A barn. A silo. A house.

One after another, like a trail of crumbs left by a child to find their way back home if they should get lost, all the clues were before me. If I just kept taking visual note of the markers below me, I'd find my way home.

Sure enough, as I returned on an extended final approach once again, there were all my reference points, aligned one after another. My way back home to safety and security was as easy as connecting point A to point B, to point C.

It's funny how things in life have a way of repeating themselves.

So much of what I've learned lately about spirituality centers on heightening the awareness of everything that is around us. The universe holds a bounty of gifts for us, if we can just become more aware of the clues. When things at first seem hopeless and you think everything is going against you, it's very easy to give up and close your eyes to any other possibility. But that's the most important time to open your eyes to the potential of a new approach.

When it comes to Parkinson's disease, doctors and researchers are working non-stop to try and find a cure. Research is about choosing to look at things differently and with an open mind, in the hopes of a new outcome.

I've chosen to do the same. I'm looking at my Parkinson's diagnosis as requiring a different approach—an approach that tells me that positive things will happen. The clues are out there. The trail to follow is, as well—for researchers and for myself.

My eyes are wide open.

CHAPTER 30

FIFTY SHAKES OF GRAY

While the creative challenge of writing a steamy, erotic Parkinson's novelette has most definitely dominated my thoughts (blame it on the dopamine agonist I take) that is not what this chapter is about. After all, cuffs present too much difficulty for us PD patients.

No, this chapter intends to focus on the gray area that ties up the thoughts of a large number of people with PD including myself: what caused their disease.

While it is known that an eighty percent loss of the dopamine-producing neurons in the brain result in the appearance of Parkinson's symptoms, the exact cause of the cell death is not understood; yet, significant research findings continue to yield important clues.

According to the National Parkinson Foundation, a few theories continue to entice researchers:

- **Free radicals** – potentially damaging molecules that are created by normal chemical reactions in the body
- **Toxins** – such as pesticides that selectively destroy dopaminergic neurons
- **Genetic factors** – While several genes are known to cause specific forms of PD, the majority of cases have no genetic link or family history of Parkinson's.

- ***Accelerated aging*** – the idea that normal, age-related wearing-away of dopamine-producing neurons occurs more rapidly in some individuals

Many researchers believe that a combination of these four factors may ultimately cause the disease.

The Michael J. Fox Foundation highlights additional risk factors based on research. For example, smoking and caffeine consumption have been associated with lower rates of Parkinson's disease, while head injury and pesticide exposure have been associated with higher risk. While such studies do not definitively link these factors with Parkinson's disease, they highlight areas where further research may lead to risk-prevention or treatment strategies.

I personally cannot stress enough how vitally important research is in finding a cure. Each of us can contribute to that process through a variety of ways:

- **Enroll in a clinical trial**. Regardless of whether you have Parkinson's or not, there are numerous clinical trials available. As you know, I am a participant in the Michael J. Fox Foundation PPMI clinical trial.
- **Fundraise**. There are countless foundations and groups that contribute to the funding of the continuation and expansion of Parkinson's research. I choose to fundraise for the National Parkinson Foundation Moving Day Chicago walk
- **Contact your politicians**. More government funding is needed. Let your representatives know you support increased funding for Parkinson's research.

The bottom line is—GET INVOLVED!

There is a Tibetan saying: "If you are too clever, you could miss the point entirely," which I interpret to mean that sometimes it's best not to overthink things—just go with your intuition.

Since I began my journaling, a significant portion of my writing has focused on my spiritual beliefs and how they are related to my Parkinson's.

In sharing my views, I have regularly mentioned that I strongly believe in intuition—listening to my gut and my heart. After all, it was a key component in helping me ultimately reach a diagnosis.

So at one point in my blogging, rather than focusing on the facts, scientific research and theory, I conducted a very unscientific survey. I asked that any willing Parkinson's patient, caretaker or loved one, respond to the following question:

What do you think caused your (or the patient's) Parkinson's disease?

I was not asking for what their doctor may have told them or what they may have read through countless articles and studies. I was strictly interested in what their *intuition* told them. I was opening a dialogue between people who share a very intimate and unique bond, and social media now allows us to easily connect and share our thoughts. Was it bad karma? Genetics? The countless cans of artificially sweetened soda you consumed? Environmental causes? Perhaps they just didn't know and the cause was irrelevant to them. There was no right or wrong answer. I simply wanted to know what they felt inside, what their inner voice or intuition told them.

Why did I want to know? Curiosity. From my conversations with people in general, I have learned numerous things in life that have been instrumental in helping open myself up to greater insight.

Parkinson's patients have a special relationship, a bond not unlike any other group of individuals that share a commonality with each other. There is a great sense of community. In private conversations with other individuals with PD and their loved ones, I've found a common, unspoken desire for a *reason*. When two individuals with PD are introduced, we're always, first and foremost, concerned for how the other person is doing. It usually starts with, "How are you doing with it?" Discussions then tend to focus on a comparison of onset of symptoms, but rarely ever cover what each of us thinks might have contributed to it. So, if for no other reason, I was offering a chance for people to share their feelings and thoughts with someone who enjoys doing the same.

Strength, frustration, confusion, depression, apathy, anger, and hope are just a few of the emotions and characteristic attitudes expressed by respondents of my survey.

There was one individual who told the exact story I have told my family ever since I was diagnosed, with eerie similarity. And there were answers I never could have imagined or hoped for. But the most unexpected reward of the survey was the profound gift it gave me in terms of a new acceptance and understanding of my disease.

The responses to the question, ***What do you believe caused your Parkinson's disease?*** were broken down into 6 distinct categories with the percentage of respondents answers listed after.

- **Pesticides/Chemicals 45%**
- **Environmental 20%**
- **Genetics/Hereditary 15%**
- **Head Trauma 7.5%**
- **Karma/Personal 7.5%**
- **Anxiety/Stress 5%**

Before providing some of the responses received, it's only fair that I answer the question as well. Although a big part of my personal acceptance of the disease is the belief that the past is unchangeable and every experience of the future can hold a new gift, it still hasn't prevented me from speculating *why*.

For me, personally, the *why* is a cocktail of three categories listed above: pesticides/chemicals, head trauma, and anxiety/stress.

Chronologically, my story goes something like this.

At the age of two or three, I was being pulled in a wagon that hit a bump in the sidewalk. I was tossed out the back end and landed on my head, resulting in an emergency room visit and twenty-six stitches in my head.

In my childhood neighborhood, as kids played outside on those never-ending summer evenings, it was customary for the mosquito abatement truck to wander through the subdivision like an ice cream truck. The fog of billowy, white pesticides flowing out of it had a strangely unique and appealing aroma. As a kid (who already had his head in the clouds), I was drawn towards that cloud, and would pretend I was tens of thousands of feet in the air instead of right there on our street.

And what about that concussion in grade school gym class? We were doing toe touches during calisthenics, and while my hands were on the floor, a classmate came up from behind, grabbed my hands from between my legs and *pulled*. I guess he thought if he pulled hard enough and quickly enough, he could spin me 360 degrees to my feet. The physics didn't work. I landed directly on my head with no hands available to break my fall. I was out cold for two minutes.

And again, two years later, while running *in* to school from recess as another student was running *out* to recess, we met—BAM!—at the corner of the building. Neither of us saw it was coming. So there you have it, three concussions within the first twelve years of my life. The number of lumps on my noggin would give a phrenologist a field day.

On to the final suspects: more chemicals. My design classes in college were filled with them, from photography classes where we developed our own prints; to graphics classes where we sometimes produced our own color pigments and dyes. Supplies in cabinets were marked with radioactive symbols, yet required no special handling on our part. Add to the list spray mounts and cleaning solvents, and that rounded out my chemical-filled education.

To me the cocktail had been mixed—it only needed to be served. Enter the stress and anxiety of running my own business for twenty-five years, plus all the other stresses of life.

How well we handle stress is very important, because it can contribute to a host of chemical and hormonal changes that can ultimately effect our cells healthy balance.

It now makes sense to me that it wasn't until my anxiety peaked to such a level that everyone saw the changes in me, that I became symptomatic. I often wonder, if I had I been better able to control my stress and let the Parkinson's "sleep", maybe it never would have woken up.

But the past is the past.

My questionnaire's statistics were rounded out by the answers I received from the rest of the respondents. Here are just a few that I would like to share.

"I believe I was on the road to a PD diagnoses in one of two ways—or maybe both, who knows. I spent a lot of time at my grandparents' cottage in Michigan growing up in the 60's and 70',s and all I drank there was well water. The other

possibility was, I spent two years overseas (1981-1983) when I was in the Air Force. I ate the fruits and veggies there from farmer's markets outside the base. God only knows what pesticides were present on that food. But I was naïve and didn't know any better at the time. Researchers say it takes a considerable amount of time for the PD to effect one enough to show symptoms, and that one is usually diagnosed after 80% of the dopamine producing cells have already died. I also believe that exercise is truly the fountain of youth and had it not been for the fact that I was always an active person, I probably would have been diagnosed sooner. But thank God I wasn't. Believe me, 45 was young enough." ~Michele H.

"My brother was diagnosed with early onset PD at age 38. He had the DBS (Deep Brain Stimulation) *surgery at approximately age 46. Intuition tells me the cause of PD is primarily environmental toxins with secondary genetic factors. My brother is a hero in my eyes. Love for his daughter and wife, plus his daily volunteer work at a rescue farm for horses, are key components in maintaining his positive spirit."* ~ Susanna S.

"I feel that my exposure to insecticides used to spray for mosquitoes when I was young caused my PD. They came around dusk and fogged the neighborhood. All the kids ran behind the truck spraying the fog. I did once, but my mother saw me, so that was the last time I did that! But every night they fogged and that fog seeped into our homes and I believe this is what did it to me. Before that, from the ages of 2 to 4, I lived on the Island of Guam (dad was in air force). I have read that the percentage of PD to amount of people there is very high, so I have always wondered if that could be how I got PD." ~Patty L.

"I've been diagnosed for 6-1/2 years. Spent a huge majority of that time on my knees. I would dearly love to know how and WHY I got this confusing and dreadful disease. My intuition is that I somehow caused it." ~Michelle P.

Not only did I read of someone with a very similar story to mine, as well as a number of individuals with entirely different theories, but I also came away with a completely new enlightenment regarding my own acceptance of Parkinson's.

We all are going to die.

I'm not simply referring to Parkinson's patients. No, I'm talking about *everyone*. We are *all* going to die. We are each on the same path, one that starts with birth and ends with death. What sets us all apart from each other and makes us each unique is what we do along that path of life. How fully we live. How well we love.

Ancient Egyptians believed that, upon their death, they would be asked two questions, and that their answers would determine whether they would continue their journey in the afterlife.

The first question was, "Did you bring joy?"

The second was, "Did you find joy?"

To me, it's all about the quality of your *living* that ultimately determines the quality of your *life*.

For some reason, after reading everyone's intuitions as to why *they* had been diagnosed with Parkinson's disease, it suddenly occurred to me that there existed another possibility as to why *I* had been diagnosed. A vast majority of us (I was guilty of this, too) go through our lives with a blind complacency. We go to work or school, come home, watch some TV, get on our computers, talk on our phones, enjoy the things we've bought, drive our cars, feed ourselves, exercise and socialize once in awhile, then go to bed, get up and do it all over again—if we're lucky. Not everyone has those luxuries, but the majority of people call that "living". It's all done without much conscious thought—almost like riding a bike. We tend to take it for granted. It's just "what we do".

Until...

Until *it* happens to either you or someone close to you that you care about.

A diagnosis.

It could be cancer, multiple sclerosis, ALS or any one of a countless number of diseases—even Parkinson's; the diagnosis is received and then you suddenly think about living—truly living.

The responses that followed this brief one-question survey were like an epiphany for me. I suddenly realized I had received a diagnosis to *live*, a personal wakeup call to decide what was important in my life. I'd been given the opportunity to make the rest of my years the *best* years of my life—ironically, with Parkinson's disease.

Some people live to the ripe old age of one hundred and have never really lived, while others are here for a much shorter time and have lived life far more fully. Some people heed the wake up call and some people don't. It's ultimately up to each individual to determine what his or her experiences will be. To me, the years are about what I do with them, not about how many I will get.

"The future is a concept, it doesn't exist. As the proverb says, tomorrow never comes. We're only really ever alive now. Bring your mind to a state of reality. Now! There is no such thing as TOMORROW. There is no past and there is no future. There never will be, because TIME is always NOW. We get distracted from living fully now by having our eye on the future. The point of life is always arrived at in the immediate moment."

I look at Parkinson's as my personal wake up call, an opportunity to really *live* my life to the fullest, day by day. My one disagreement with the above proverb is that, for Parkinson's, there is a tomorrow, and the disease will continue to affect others. I do have to recognize that, and continue to help fight against it until Parkinson's has no tomorrow and it has no today.

Did I bring joy? Did I find joy?

We shall see.

CHAPTER 31

CARE TO STEP OUTSIDE?

"Let your mind start a journey through a strange new world. Leave all thoughts of the world you knew before. Let your soul take you where you long to be... Close your eyes let your spirit start to soar, and you'll live as you've never lived before."

~ Erich Fromm

At the wonderfully inquisitive age of five, my son Adam once asked me what kind of work I did when I went to my office every day. Happy that my son was taking an interest in my job, I proudly replied, "I'm a Graphic Designer. I design packaging, brochures and logos for companies that pay me to do so."

Adam looked at me with a blank stare that made it obvious he hadn't a clue about anything I had just said.

"I draw and color, Adam," I explained, taking a much simpler approach.

To which my son replied, "That's not a job Dad. We do that in kindergarten."

Truth told, while my four years in Art and Design at the University of Illinois were instrumental in refining my talents and preparing me for running my own design agency, my single year of kindergarten was quite possibly the most developmentally important year of my life. Not only did I acquire a basic skill set for my future career, but also more importantly it started me down a path toward mastering a skill that would ultimately allow me to deal with my Parkinson's disease in such a positive manner.

The skill was creativity.

My kindergarten exuberance was over the opportunity to have the brand new box of Crayola crayons with the built-in sharpener. The smell of the fresh wax when you first opened the box was one of those scents you remember all of your life. There were only a few other aromas I remember so vividly from my childhood: Playdoh, Vicks Vapo-Rub, mothballs and Wind Song perfume—the last two were only available at my grandmother's house. But the crayons were something special.

That pristine box of coloring sticks held all the creative potential this five-year-old needed. Whether it would be fire trucks ablaze in Crimson Red, or dolphins swimming in oceans of Cerulean Blue, I knew that box held the opportunity for me to escape into an imaginary world. Those crayons represented hours of fun in the playground of my mind. Creativity allowed me to see my world differently. It was never in short supply.

At sixteen years of age, my close high school friends and I had exhausted our standard fare of summertime activities such as movies, parties and hanging out at the mall, so we decided to do something a little—shall we say—creative.

A group of eight of us pooled our money, rented a full stretch limousine, and donned some of our finest seventies wear for a night out on the town. Now for those of you who didn't grow up in the seventies, "donning your finest seventies wear" was a bigger stretch than the limo itself. Those clothes were awful. For the times, however, we looked pretty groovy, and on this particular 1976 summer night, we had to make an impression.

Our plan was to pretend we were an upstart rock band, setting out on tour to promote the release of our brand new album. We had even gone so far as to scour the local used record stores for the most obscure band we could find (which turned out to be of a Dutch progressive rock band called Solution), bought their one available album and shrink wrapped it to appear as our own. We outfitted our stretch limo with my mom's white princess phone and loaded in a menagerie of musical instruments.

Three more friends who were part of the charade were scheduled to be at a local movie theater—two laden with flash bulb cameras and another as a reporter with a microphone for on-site interviews. (All of this at a time when Ashton Kutcher and Punk'd were still a dream away.)

We accomplished the "set-up" by pulling up to the theater and informing the manager that we were there for the press announcement to promote our new album. After the flustered young man reported to us that nothing had been scheduled in his book, and we had called our agent on our useless princess phone to complain (thereby enhancing our ruse), we asked the manager for the timing of all the movie end times so we would know exactly when the patrons would be filing out. He obliged us with the details for every movie. Everything was set.

Our entourage pulled up to the curb with precision timing as streams of teenagers began to file out of the theater.

With a driver's cap adorning his head, our chauffeur swung open the doors of our limo and we stepped out into the brilliance of flashing lights and curious gawks by teenage girls. After a few phony interviews discussing our fictitious upcoming concert, we used the lure of free concert tickets and the opportunity to appear on our next album, to entice some of the girls to pose with us in pictures.

When a snap of our fingers to the chauffeur was met with the embarrassed revelation that our agent had forgotten to give him the tickets, we were left with no other choice than to take down the names and phone numbers of dozens of cute teenage girls so that we could call them later and get the tickets to them ourselves.

Now *that* was creativity—and allowing myself to believe that anything was possible.

In design school they reinforced what I had already been putting into practice all my life, that to be creative you needed to allow yourself to think outside of the box. In essence, you needed to throw out the rules of the reality you've come to accept for yourself. When it comes to creativity, there are no rules.

A simple example was a college design project where we were asked to design a Seasons Greetings holiday card. We were asked to imagine that, instead of a snowflake being frozen water in crystalline form, what if they looked like ping pong balls? Or eggs? Or marshmallows? How would it affect your design? How would it affect the solution?

What I am discovering is that very same skill they were teaching in design school is something I have been practicing all my life. Creativity. Learning to look at things in a different way. Redefining my reality. Suspending my beliefs.

Just like the snowflakes project, why does Parkinson's have to look a certain way? Why do I, as a Parkinson's patient, have to be effected by it in a certain way? What if I choose to change the perspective on it one hundred eighty degrees and see it entirely different? In combination with what my doctors are doing for me, I'm willing to take a prescription of positive thinking. Through the very simple act of redefining my patient role, I am now in control; Parkinson's is not in control of me.

I chose at the moment of my diagnosis to step outside of myself and become the observer of me with Parkinson's, not the patient being observed. From an outside perspective, I was going to be the art director of this Parkinson's project and actively design what I want my Parkinson's to be. I am designing the solution by redefining the problem.

I've given myself that brand new box of crayons, and I'm coloring my Parkinson's world a bright Sunshine Yellow.

Maybe I did learn everything I needed to know in kindergarten.

Thank you, Mrs. Cannon.

CHAPTER 32

CAN I GET FRIES WITH THIS SHAKE?

After receiving my diagnosis of Parkinson's, work was most definitely top of mind. I immediately started thinking about how the disease might impact my design business as well as my ability to work in general. My first reaction was to throw out the martini-shaker joke, but that lightheartedness was meant to compensate for the fear of knowing deep down that it does often adversely affect a person's ability to work.

According to the National Parkinson Foundation, it is estimated that twenty-five to thirty-five percent of people diagnosed with PD are still active in the workforce. To me, that number seemed incredibly small. I had been hoping to read that a good fifty percent were still working. Maybe there was more value in my humor after all.

I am at a slight advantage for being able to contribute toward increasing that statistic, since I own my own business and am the sole employee. I'm pretty sure that the chances that someone within my company would discriminate against me are pretty slim. And if he does, I'll fire him. But discrimination does exist within other companies.

According to the NPF, if you believe your company is one that might discriminate against someone with a disability, you are not legally required to mention your PD diagnosis to your employer as long as you can adequately perform your work. For additional information regarding The Americans with Disabilities Act, visit www.ada.gov or www.dol.gov/odep/.

Of equal concern to me was how my clients might react. I can't control that kind of discrimination. If I were to let clients know, might they think I am no longer as capable as I once was? After all, it's a creative field and it takes a creative mind to design Since Parkinson's is disease of the brain, it's possible that they might think my creativity has been affected as well.

Sounds ludicrous?

On more than one occasion, while explaining to someone that my Parkinson's presently manifests itself through slowness of movement, people have responded by saying, "Well, does it help if I talk slower for you?" or, "Does your brain have a hard time keeping up with the rest of us who are talking faster?"

I usually just respond with "Yeah, talk slow, and can I get fries with this shake?"

I used to work at McDonalds. In 1976, my friend Patrick took a job there and talked me into putting in an application. However, as soon as I was hired, Patrick quit. I was left there for a year to work the fry machine—just what every sixteen-year-old's dermatologist recommends for a clear complexion.

The funny thing about the McDonalds job, and the same was true for my stint as assistant manager of Papa Del's Pizza restaurant in college, if you had to go somewhere right after work and you didn't have time to run home, shower and change, you could walk into any party or gathering and inevitably hear, "Did somebody bring McDonalds?" or "Who's got the pizza?" It certainly was not a chick magnet but I was quite popular with the pet of the house.

My very first job was working for my pediatrician at the age of fourteen. I cleaned the patient offices, prepared the doctor's charts for the following day and polished the floors.

Over the years I have sold Christmas trees at a garden center, worked in the food service department of the local hospital, was a front desk clerk for the Hyatt hotels, took care of a fleet of service trucks for the natural gas company in the area, canvassed neighborhoods for public action committees, baby sat, cut lawns, delivered newspapers and painted houses.

I was never a stranger to work, and I plan on continuing to work for a long time. In fact, I've already started to put together a list of jobs (besides those already mentioned) where my Parkinson's symptoms will put me at the top of the potential candidates:

- Snow Globe Salesman (tremor)
- Librarian (dysarthria; low voice volume)
- Doctor (micrographia; illegible handwriting)
- Road Repair Crew (bradykinesia; slowness of movement)
- DMV (bradykinesia; slowness of movement)

In all seriousness, on more than one occasion I've thought it would be great to put together a business that utilized the unique skill set of Parkinson's patients so that we could always be employed—a place where our disabilities provide the opportunity.

Let's work on that.

CHAPTER 33

WHISTLE WHILE YOU TWERK

With the world's technology rapidly evolving, new products come to market faster than we can adapt to using them all. For the most part, we are left to pick and choose which suit our particular needs best, or we follow cultural trends of those technologies that are generating the most buzz.

Take, for example, my field of graphic design. Bigger, faster, brighter, sleeker, smarter, thinner, cheaper and more powerful computers are released with greater frequency each passing year. With my most recent computer purchase, by the time I had unpacked the box and figured out where to plug my mouse cord in, Apple had introduced a cordless mouse. My computer was already antiquated and I hadn't even figured out what my eight-character-one-capital-letter-one-number-one punctuation-mark login password was going to be.

And that's just the hardware; the software updates come even quicker. The mere thought of actually being able to go through all the functionality updates and to do all the tutorials that come with a new system is a joke. I have some *real* work to do, after all.

As if the speed at which new technology is coming at us isn't bad enough, add in our constantly changing language. I honestly just found out what *twerking* is from my daughters, around the same time that I discovered my son was upstairs doing a *selfie*. Had my kids told me they were doing these things without further explanation, I probably would have said, "Just make sure you keep your doors closed and the blinds pulled down."

Yes, change is definitely happening faster, at a time when I am physically becoming slower. Parkinson's is certainly not technology friendly.

The area of greatest struggle for me is writing, be it handwriting or typing on the keyboard. (That last sentence alone took me roughly seven hours to type.) Trust me, Parkinson's limitations make writing these chapters a monumental accomplishment. My hands move clumsily across the keyboard and my fingers feel heavy and stiff. I once was very proud of the speed at which I could type with just two fingers, but that has slowed dramatically. Some times are better than others depending on how well my meds are "on". There are occasions where everything seems perfectly normal. At other times, my fingers can barely push down the keys. I may rest a hand on the keyboard and periodic spasms in my fingers end up pushing the space bar an extra twenty times.

My penmanship is effected in just about the same way. When my hands are stiff, my writing becomes clumsy, fatigued and illegible. The next day, there may be no discernable problems at all.

The symptom as associated with Parkinson's disease is called "micrographia", and is characterized by abnormally small, cramped handwriting or the progression to continually smaller handwriting. It's cause, according to the National Parkinson Foundation, is attributed to a common feature of PD, which is a slowing of movement in general, and muscle stiffness in the hands and fingers. Loss of automatic motion affects the easy, flowing motion of handwriting. This can impact even simple writing tasks such as signing your name.

This started me thinking...

Parkinson's disease is named after the English doctor James Parkinson, who published the first detailed description of symptoms in *An Essay on the Shaking Palsy* in 1817.

In 1817!

Might there be any signatures of record prior to 1817 that show signs of a typical Parkinson's style of writing?

Of what importance was that to me? Well, my entire attitude around my diagnosis of Parkinson's has been about succeeding with the disease by maintaining positivity about it. I was curious if there might be individuals who had continued to achieve and possibly even make a mark in history while in the midst of dealing with PD, at a time when they didn't have today's technology, support or treatments. Obviously, this was all pure speculation because, prior to 1817, it was not classified as Parkinson's; but I was curious, nonetheless.

The first thing I did was to Google "micrographia", thinking I might find a visual example of the malady that I could use for comparison to any earlier documents I might come across. Sure enough, there on Wikipedia was a writing example of a Parkinson's patient.

The next step was to begin searching documents prior to 1817 that might offer a similar writing style. I was not going to go about this by pure happenstance; on the contrary. I had a hunch and I had definite place in mind to start. There was one document in particular I wanted to take a look at, and sure enough, my intuition was correct.

Stephen Hopkins, a Rhode Island delegate to the First Continental Congress, signed the Declaration of Independence. In the summer of 1776, while holding his right hand with his left, he is quoted as saying, "Although my hand trembles, my heart does not," and he signed that famous document.

Here was my "proof", my individual of notoriety, that I felt had that characteristic signature during an era when the flourish ornate signatures were an art form of the day.

Here was a man among men. Stephen Hopkins, born in 1707 and died in 1785 at the age of seventy-eight. He came from a prominent Rhode Island family and most definitely left his mark upon a nation. Not only did my initial examination of the document serve to heighten my belief, further research into his biography removed all doubt. His own admission was proof enough for me.

It gave me tremendous pause to sit and look at that Declaration of Independence and those signatures and consider what thoughts must have been going through Stephen Hopkins' mind. I imagine that he had a sense of uncertainty for what the future held for our new country at that time, but was probably, simultaneously, dealing with the uncertainty of and concern for his own health. He held the same questions in his mind then about his health that millions still hold to this day: *What is causing this? What can be done?*

As I reread that simple quote of Stephen Hopkins, a number of thoughts came to mind. First, I felt a tremendous amount of respect for the man because he was not afraid to share with his friends and colleagues the disease that afflicted him, especially at a time when there was no explanation he could offer for what ailed him. He openly acknowledged his tremor and in doing so, implied he was not ashamed of it. Second, he had not allowed his tremor or the disease to limit him. He had continued on with his passion for his work.

Most profound was the double meaning I took from his words as a whole. Obviously in literal context, he was referring to our young nation, and "though (his) hand trembles" while signing this Declaration of Independence, "(his) heart does not." He believed this important document to be the right direction for his country. However, the other context could refer to the tremorous disease itself. His words become an analogy to how I have felt all along: "Although my hand trembles, my heart does not." It's that strange sense of positivity shining through, that I can deal with whatever life brings me.

Today, more than two hundred years later, technology is most definitely moving at a rapid pace, as is research being done toward finding a cure for Parkinson's. To continue that work and to hasten the success, additional funding is always needed. Volunteers and foundations continue to spearhead the vast majority of the fundraising efforts, but more needs to be done.

I find it extremely ironic that the first example of this kind of signature I found belonged to a statesman, a member of the First Continental Congress; because additional support and funding from our government is desperately needed to keep progress moving forward and to ultimately find a cure. I ask that everyone reading this to take the opportunity to write your Congressman—with a steady hand—to request that they show the heart of our founding fathers and support increased funding for Parkinson's research.

Reblog it. ReTweet it. Do it for your selfie. Or for someone you love.

CHAPTER 34

BAH HUMBUG

As a child growing up in Chicago in the 1960s, there were a handful of TV shows that I would consider staples of my childhood. On the weekdays, if I was home sick from school, it was *Bozo the Clown*, followed by *Bewitched* and *Leave it to Beaver*. On Saturdays, I was up at 7 a.m. to watch an endless stream of cartoons like *Bugs Bunny*, *Road Runner* and *Casper*, just to name a few. Later on Saturday night, if my parents went out, I could watch *Creature Features* with the babysitter.

Creature Features were the classic monster movies of Frankenstein, Wolf man, Dracula and The Mummy. Our babysitter would let us watch them and then in the middle of the night I'd wake my parents after having a bad dream.

But the best memory of all was shown on Sunday television.

Sundays at my grandmother's house meant a late afternoon dinner of homemade roast beef with dumplings or mashed potatoes, a vegetable I hated, and chocolate cream pie for dessert. It also meant a TV show called *Family Classics,* which aired classic Hollywood movies the entire family could enjoy. Shortly after dinner, everyone would all gather around the TV set in the living room as the melodic theme music began to play. The host, Frazier Thomas, would enter the small set which was designed to look like the personal library in a prosperous home along Chicago's north shore. An ornate, high back chair sat next to an end table and lamp, and hundreds of leather bound volumes filled a bookcase in the background. Each book title corresponded to a movie that might be featured that night.

At the start of the show, Frazier would take a book off the shelf and preface the movie with details about locale, characters and plot, eventually revealing the title. *Moby Dick* starring Gregory Peck, *National Velvet* with a young Elizabeth Taylor or *Heidi* with Shirley Temple in the lead role, could be any one of the books he might pull from the shelf.

This recollection of my childhood Sundays reminded me of one of those cinematic classics that shared some very unique similarities to my Parkinson's disease.

The movie? Charles Dickens' *A Christmas Carol*.

Like Scrooge's visit from the third and final spirit, I, too, have been given the opportunity to have a glimpse of my future. I guess you could say I have had a visit from the Ghost of Parkinson's Yet To Come.

While Scrooge would be taken on a journey that would show him how he is viewed by others, ultimately left trembling in realization of the awful person he had become, my vision showed me who I might become and how I might be viewed by others, all as a result of my trembling.

My visits with this Ghost of Parkinson's Yet To Come have been repeated over the last few weeks as I've sat at my keyboard working on a design project or typing, as I am now. Working at my computer, I will periodically rest my left arm on the arm of the chair just to give my fatigued hands and fingers a chance to rest as I proofread copy or look over a design. One day I noticed that the pinky finger of my left hand had started to twitch. I stared at it for a few seconds, watching as it moved ever so slightly but with a rhythm like a metronome, as if it were trying to keep to a beat. I observed with a strange sense of detachment, as if I were learning about tremor through this chance observation. There was no sense of fear or panic on my part; but more like a sense of wonder.

My primary symptoms of Parkinson's to date had been slowness of movement, so the introduction of a tremor was definitely the first new sign of any progression in my condition over the past two years. Additionally, the tremor had become visible when I would execute fine motor skills with my left hand, like trying to pick up a paperclip or other small object. As I would pick up the object, the fingers holding the item would begin to shake., but once I put it down, flex the fingers, and the tremor would subside.

Unlike a persistent tremor, my tremor is presently transient, only occurring every now and then, hence my analogy that it has been making "visits" to me rather than taking up permanent residency. It's apparently checking out the living space and making future plans to move in.

Unfortunately, Parkinson's disease doesn't have a consistent set of symptoms for each individual it impacts. One person may develop a tremor, while the next person may not. As a result, each PD patient is left to contemplate the ways in which Parkinson's will change his or her life. The hardest part is not knowing what might be around the next corner; not knowing what you can prepare for; not knowing what you can rule out.

What you can try to do is follow my lead and meet the future, in whatever form that it might take, with a positive attitude.

Ebenezer Scrooge quite accurately captures my feelings about meeting my uninvited guest, my Ghost of Parkinson's Yet To Come, when he says, "Ghost of the Future, I fear you more than any spectre I have seen. But as I know your purpose is to do me good, and as I hope to live to be another man from what I was, I am prepared to bear you company, and do it with a thankful heart."

CHAPTER 35

CAREGIVER, REDEFINED

I thought I knew what a caregiver was. After all, I am a male.

I was pretty sure I had a caregiver ever since I was born. The first was my mother, and the second, my wife. Why, there may have even been a few others who considered themselves caregivers with all the whining I did while growing up. Although my mother and wife might beg to differ with me, these people were not caregivers, not in the truest meaning of the word, as I want to pay homage to today.

Until recently, I hadn't any appreciation for the selfless dedication and sacrifice a true caregiver makes on behalf of a loved one or patient; nor the kind of stress and emotional toll they undergo. I didn't understand the isolation which caregivers often endure when committing their time to the care of another.

About four years ago, my father-in-law's illness took a turn for the worse, which made it necessary for him to have consistent in-home care. From that point on, I saw firsthand what a caregiver provides, endures and sacrifices when they care for someone who is ill.

Alvin was the man who, for the last two years of my father-in-law's life, formed a partnership with him on behalf of his failing body. He was truly an angel from above. Through observing not only the partnership that formed but the friendship as well, I clearly came to know, understand and appreciate what a caregiver is.

Not only did Alvin attend to all of my father-in-law's physical needs, like bathing, feeding, and dressing him with an incredible sense of dignity and respect. He also helped him maintain a connection with the outside world, which was so strongly defined by his family, friendships, business and social opportunities. It was not uncommon, after bathing and dressing my father-in-law each morning, for Alvin to take him to his former place of business, the company he founded, providing him the important sense of still being connected to his world, regardless of his physical limitations. Alvin recognized the importance of that human need for contact. Afterwards, Alvin might take my father-in-law out to lunch, either by themselves or to meet with friends. He would take pictures of their adventure and send them via text to each of my father-in-law's children, along with a note: "Dad's doing ok. We're having a good day." It meant the world to my wife and to her brother and sister.

It was so clear to me that this was not just a job—Alvin cared.

Alvin was also there with my father-in-law on the day that things were not so good. The day my father-in-law died. On that day, he provided a hand to hold, a feeling of connection for as long as was needed—and when my father-in-law was ready to let go, he helped him do it with dignity and respect.

Alvin cared. And Alvin cried.

The definition of a caregiver, according to the Webster's Dictionary, is "a person who provides aide, assistance or direct care to someone who is sick." To me, the term *care* in this definition sounds like a mere product or a service. Caregivers are so much more than that. What it fails to define is the unique attribute of a caregiver's spirit or soul.

I would like to offer my own definition: A caregiver is a person who **cares** enough for others to be able to **give** of one's self. In this way, *care* no longer implies a product or service, but rather a quality of the individual's heart. To care enough about someone is a choice driven by emotion and a common sense of humanity. It also acknowledges the incredible sacrifice caregivers make out of love for another being—their willingness to give of themselves to another.

Empathy is one of the highest expressions of love. It acknowledges one's willingness to take on someone else's pain.

No matter how you choose to define the term, there is no denying that—by the very nature of the work they do, be it by choice or by circumstance—caregivers embody love and kindness, and make incredible personal sacrifices each day out of a true sense of caring.

Eighteen months prior to my father-in-law's passing, I was diagnosed with Parkinson's disease. When I first received the diagnosis, I immediately thought of my father-in-law and wondered if Parkinson's might run a similar course for me. Was I going to become reliant on someone for all of my daily needs? With that thought came an overwhelming concern for my wife and my children. I didn't want my health to be the cause of their lives being turned upside down. I never wanted to be a burden. While I felt determined that I would manage whatever PD would challenge me with, I didn't want it to be *their* challenge.

Since then I have come to learn that, as patients, we must remember we are not the only ones who are impacted by our disease, but that our caregivers need to be cared for, as well.

If you're someone who has the capability and capacity to offer your help to a caregiver, even if it's to provide them some personal time for only a few hours—please offer. Just remember, by definition it's really pretty simple to do; *Care* enough for others to be able to *give* of one's self.

CHAPTER 36

PARKINSON'S DISEASE IS NOT A NOUN

It probably won't come as much of a surprise for me to admit that I haven't had any formal training as a writer, whatsoever. I haven't had any formal training with Parkinson's disease either. They each just happen to be hobbies I've recently taken up and, for the most part, I'm refining my skills with both as I go along.

When I think back to my high school English classes and the creative writing papers we were required to compose, all I recall is how they were returned to me with more red ink on them then the indigo or ebony I submitted them with. How was that possible? You would think that the teacher would be limited to just writing her critique between the lines of my prose; but no, *my* teachers would reach the end of the paper and then draw arrows instructing me that they were continuing on the back. *Rude!* It quite often had something to do with run-on sentences, participles that were left dangling or improper usage of a verb, an adverb or a proverb. And I definitely remember my teachers saying you can't start a sentence with the word "and."

What astounded me the most, was the fact that I was truly trying my best—and I really felt good about my efforts. The style I was putting forth was comfortable to me. My papers were conversational. I knew I was "doing it wrong", but I just couldn't figure out a way to change and still be true to myself in the end.

Something similar has happened to me with Parkinson's.

The Webster's dictionary says "Parkinson's disease" is a noun. It's not. It's a conjunction, like "and", "but", "or", "nor", "for", "so", or "yet". It's a *joiner*, used to bring things together. At least that's what it has been to me.

For me Parkinson's disease has meant a connection. A connection to my childhood and rediscovering events that relate to today. It's a connection to a community of Parkinson's patients and the people that love them, through fundraising initiatives like Moving Day Chicago. It's a connection to humanity as I partake in the PPMI clinical study with the Michael J. Fox Foundation. It's brought about a reconnection to my spirituality, the force behind my positive attitude toward PD. And most importantly, it has ensured a forever connection with my children through my writings about who I am and what I am about.

Like any good creative writing paper, Parkinson's disease also has irony. Not only does Parkinson's hold the potential to create connections for people—it holds the equal capability of disrupting or destroying connections.

By definition, Parkinson's disease is the deterioration of connections in the brain. It's the continual loss of dopamine, which is the chemical messenger or neurotransmitter responsible for transmitting signals critical to produce smooth, purposeful movement. Loss of dopamine results in abnormal, nerve-firing connections within the brain that cause impaired movement.

That's the medical malady.

Unfortunately, Parkinson's has proven equally capable at disrupting the connections outside of my body—the very connections I was hoping to strengthen.

From the very beginning I have repeatedly said I never wanted to be defined by Parkinson's. Yet that is exactly what has happened, and the only person I have to blame is myself. From the combination of my involvement and dedication to fundraising for Parkinson's disease; to my excitement over my participation in the Michael J Fox Foundation's PPMI clinical study; to my rediscovery of my spirituality as it relates to my positive attitude; and finally my immersion into writing my blog and now my book—I have defined myself as Parkinson's. I see myself as Parkinson's. My friends see me as Parkinson's. My family sees me as Parkinson's. I guess I haven't given them any other choice.

I suppose my connection to Parkinson's now borders on obsessive, yet to me it's always been a positive obsession. It gives me strength to know I am taking an active role in fighting this disease and hopefully contributing toward its cure. It excites me to be able to partner with others in that same passion. I am relishing in my spirituality and I have such a positive vision of things to come that I love sharing it. However, I recognize that it's not easy for those closest to me to understand that obsessive passion.

It's similar to what I wrote about above, regarding my high school composition papers: *I just couldn't figure out the way to make a change and still be true to my self in the end.*

My family has been incredibly supportive and loving. They appreciate my passion and understand my dedication. They also yearn for some time with the husband and father that Parkinson's was not going to define.

I have no plans of making any drastic changes towards my dedication to eradicate Parkinson's or change what I need to do to help myself in managing the disease. I will continue to fundraise aggressively, remain dedicated to my involvement in clinical trials, and write passionately about my experiences. But I recognize that I need to refocus and rededicate myself to the ideal that Parkinson's will not define me.

I will redefine Parkinson's: from a noun to a conjunction.

It's time to reconnect.

CHAPTER 37

HEART FOR HEART'S SAKE

"The healthy love of oneself is a great religious value. The person who does not love himself will not be able to love anybody else, ever. The first ripple of love has to rise in your heart. If it has not risen for yourself it cannot rise for anybody else, because everybody else is farther away from you.

"It is like throwing a stone in the silent lake—the first ripples will arise around the stone and then they will go on spreading to the further shores. The first ripple of love has to be around yourself." ~ Osho

After just having finished another remarkable healing session with my massage therapist, Staci Page, I felt compelled to put into words what it is that makes her sessions so unique and beneficial. While the cliché expression would be to describe what she does as "nothing short of magical", the more accurate description is that she accomplishes nothing short of spiritual.

The name of Staci's practice is Take Sanctuary. Staci not only heals through multiple modes of therapy, but she is both an artist who paints, and an artiste at her healing craft. Her business is located in the shadows of Northwestern University on the shores of Lake Michigan, just north of Chicago in Evanston, Illinois—very appropriate, in that both the University and Staci's practice epitomize excellence at the highest levels of education. Staci has trained and refined her abilities for over seventeen years now, and her vast knowledge is apparent.

Staci's website describes, in great detail, her services, the benefits and the types of clients that are a good fit for her, all important aspects when choosing a therapist.

What I find to be of utmost importance is the description of her intent: To assist her clients in discovering **how to live extraordinary lives that they love, and go on to help others make a difference in the world.**

What a fantastic business plan!

Like the opening to this chapter, Staci Page recognizes that the first ripple of love has to be around oneself. When you can discover how to love yourself, then you can change the world, and Staci offers assistance toward accomplishing that. Now treating yourself to a massage could most definitely be considered a way of showing love for your self, but the healing that Staci offers goes far beyond that.

By all outward appearances, Staci would appear to be your typical massage therapist. No, strike that, she would appear to be more of your typical soccer mom (because she is one). She's a wife and mother of two children who also happens to have a remarkable gift as a healer.

I first sought out Staci's services a little over a year-and-a-half ago, around the time I was first diagnosed with Parkinson's disease. I had read that massage therapy showed positive benefits for PD patients, and I was looking to put everything into my arsenal that was possible for combating this disease. Being a small business owner, I had long been a proponent of massage therapy, having routinely received massages in the past for stress management. However, due to personal financial cutbacks I chose to make, massage was a "luxury" I hadn't afforded myself for some time.

The services Staci offers should not be viewed as a luxury that someone provides themself with once in a while, any more than seeing their general physician or their dentist would be. Staci provides healing and health maintenance, both on the physical level and spiritual level. While she utilizes some typical pressure massage techniques in her work, and is fully trained in that mode, her massage sessions are anything but typical. They are transformational.

I personally had never experienced anything except what most would view as a conventional massage. For me, a massage meant an opportunity to relax and have a physical therapist work on muscle tension and pain in my physical body. The extent of conversation would usually be, "I feel a tightness in my neck or lower back," and the therapist would do their best to work out the knots. A really good massage therapist was one who was intuitive enough to find the knots on their own, and skilled enough at relieving them so as not to leave me in pain from the massage the following day. Those kind of massage benefits, however, were very short lived, and the greatest positive effects were often just felt in the moment. It was a very one-sided relationship where my involvement in my healing didn't go beyond my initial instructions of where I hurt, and the therapist's healing didn't go beyond the muscle and fascia.

There is so much farther someone can go.

Staci Page does much more than manipulate muscle and tissue for the purposes of healing. Staci is a facilitator. She creates a healing partnership with her client and promotes personal transformation that heals both physically and spiritually—a healing of the complete person. She does it by facilitating dialogue and spiritual growth.

In the same way someone would care for a plant, every so often you need to change the soil and provide food for maximum growth to take place. It needs to bask in the sunshine. Though strong roots may be established, without providing them room to grow and the nourishment to sustain that growth, its full beauty might never be realized.

Similarly, Staci opens doors to personal growth by helping her clients rediscover and transform their lives. She provides spiritual nourishment and the opportunity for a change in one's environment, empowering each client to discover their complete potential; to realize their full beauty. The extent of her touch goes far beyond the skin or even deep tissue, and reaches areas of great need in one's spirit. She's not working magic, but she most definitely has a gift for helping people heal themselves.

From the moment you are first greeted by Staci and her warm smile, the entire session is a dialogue, whether words are spoken or not. A typical session begins with an inquiry as to how you are feeling and what question you are holding, meaning: What is the predominant thought you are carrying in your heart, mind or gut? What would you like to resolve? Once you are on the massage table, Staci employs various techniques including craniosacral therapy and other hands-on healing arts modalities that resonate throughout your whole being. Due to her education in shamanic healing practices, Staci often provides a very spiritual dialogue as well.

After my hour-and-a-half session, we usually conclude with a more in-depth dialogue. I share feelings, emotions and thoughts about my life, and I quite often have profound epiphanies that have a lasting effect. In that regard, so much of Staci's physical work and emotional healing continues long after the session. Her insight and personal enlightenment energize me both physically and spiritually, and the positive impact on my Parkinson's has been remarkable.

One day, such an epiphany took place. As I had mentioned earlier, Staci is an incredibly talented painter as well. It is another of her many gifts. You may recall that she had created a painting for me after one of our earlier sessions. It was a simple, soulfully inspired blue circle around a lavender heart. For the longest time, contemplating its symbolism occupied my thoughts. Staci had explained that her paintings are often inspired by her visions with no direct meaning to her, but are meant for personal interpretation by the recipient.

Well, on this day, I discovered my answer. It was the last line of the quote that I began this chapter with, and it's the intent of Take Sanctuary as a practice: "The first ripple of love has to be around yourself." Love your life and you can change the world.

Staci's been helping me change my world by helping me live an extraordinary life that I love. Thank you, Staci, from the bottom of my heart.

CHAPTER 38

FREUDIAN SLIP OR SPANX®?

"One day, in retrospect, the years of struggle will strike you as the most beautiful." ~Sigmund Freud

I'm purely guessing here, but I think Sigmund Freud and possibly Frazier Crane may have been the only two individuals who have successfully conducted psychotherapy on themselves. While I am most definitely seeing positive results from the cathartic process of journaling my thoughts and experiences with Parkinson's disease and spirituality, at times I ponder if I am coming up with more answers for myself, or more questions.

When I first began writing TITU (*Tremors in the Universe*—oh, come on, everyone else has an acronym!), one of the primary reasons was for personal therapy, that by going through the process of writing down my feelings and observations, I might be able to shed some light on why and how I have come to be blessed with this positive outlook on Parkinson's.

So how do you feel you are doing, Robert?

Well, as far as any breakthroughs or major progress goes, the first thing I know for sure is that the recurring dream of walking naked into a public place that almost all people have, has definitely become a reality for me. You know the one, the dream where you're scrambling down the aisle of the grocery to hide behind the cucumber display because you suddenly realize that, in your haste to take advantage of free sample day, you ran out of the house and neglected to put a stitch of clothing on—and now someone's calling for a price check on baby gherkins. That is exactly what it has been like to bare my soul to everyone as I share my most intimate thoughts and feelings about my childhood, my spirituality and my Parkinson's disease.

Everyone DOES have that dream, right?

Regardless, I'm fortunate that this is nothing more than a personal journal of my thoughts intended for therapy, and that I only have two readers: The nice man from Nigeria who sends me emails about the large sums of money he's going to transfer when I can get around to sending him my bank account information; and the very sweet little old lady who goes by the name "C. Alice" who is apparently confused and thinks my problem is ED (erectile dysfunction) and not PD.

Come to think of it, it *would* explain my dream and my tendency to hide behind the cucumbers.

The journaling process has actually been tremendously therapeutic, and as a result, I feel I've arrived at a better understanding of where my positive attitude comes from. The "how" and "why" remain a mystery.

To successfully arrive at an answer, any self-analyzing therapist worth their weight in nuts would need a couch to lie down on for quality introspection. At least that's what I had at first assumed. However, I've quickly discovered that my treadmill works just fine for the very same purpose.

What once was a piece of exercise equipment in my arsenal of Parkinson's-fighting weaponry, has morphed into the equivalent of a therapist's couch, a yoga mat for meditation, a diagnostic tool for my Parkinson's symptoms and my creative place for writing. It truly has become quite the utilitarian vehicle.

On my treadmill at 5:00 a.m. each morning, I feel like Forrest Gump. You know, the scene where Forrest decides to run across the United States? And when he reaches the ocean, he figures since he'd got that far he might as well turn around and run back across to the other ocean? And then when he gets to the other ocean, he figures since he'd got that far he might as well turn around and keep on going?

That's me. I'm Forrest Gump.

At that time of the morning there is very little rational thought in my mind. I'm just happy to be moving. I know moving is important to my health, so I move—and I keep moving, with very little thought. Eventually I gain consciousness. Then I'm on the clock and my therapy begins.

The greatest benefit I've discovered from my morning treadmill therapy is its effectiveness in treating my PMS. *What? You think it's impossible for me to have problems with PMS?* Not at all! (I was born in February and am an Aquarius. After all, Aquarians are known for retaining water.) However, the PMS I am referring to is my Physical, Mental and Spiritual well-being.

The physical aspect of my routine is really quite simple. The first step is to do a physical assessment of how my body feels each morning. Getting on the treadmill first thing is a great Parkinson's barometer. It's like a pilot doing a pre-flight walk around of an airplane before taking off, only, in my case I'm assessing the condition of my body before starting my day. As I walk on the treadmill, I gauge whether my balance is good that morning or if I'm listing to one side like the Titanic. If I'm leaning a bit, then I'll hold onto the handrails until I feel my balance and stability return. Even on the days I feel a little bit physically "off" (and as long as I've had a good night's sleep), after a few minutes on the treadmill, I feel a sense of normalcy return.

My primary goal is to be on the treadmill every single day. By making exercise routine and doing it daily, I gain a wonderful psychological benefit. Although it may not be medically or scientifically possible, it's my creative way of thinking that as long as I continue training my brain to work those muscles daily, the ability to walk will always be second nature—just like riding a bike. Then, when the dopamine and normal connections are no longer there, my brain's *memory* of how to walk will take over.

Just keep moving.

Beyond that, I try to get in at least forty-five minutes to an hour of additional exercise every morning: a good pace, a good sweat, burn some calories and provide enough time for me to complete the rest of my "head-mill" therapy.

"It is what it is."

Whenever I write that out, look at it, and recite it in my head, I hear James Earl Jones saying it in a God-like voice, as if he were on Mount Sinai in the movie *The Ten Commandments* saying it to Moses.

"It is what it is" has been my mantra from the very moment that I had a confirmed Parkinson's diagnosis. I've had a remarkable sense of acceptance, coupled with a strong intuition that everything would be ok, which has given rise to my very positive outlook and sense of calm. It means that what's in the past cannot be changed, and the only thing that matters is the present and the future.

I'm not a person who likes dwelling on the past. The past is history —a series of facts that I cannot change. The fact that I was presented with on July 12th, 2012, is I have Parkinson's; but there weren't any facts that said Parkinson's will absolutely be this or absolutely be that. And I'm certainly not going to allow my outlook on life to be altered by mere speculation. When given the choice of how I wanted to think about my present and future with Parkinson's, I chose to only focus on the positives—the negatives would do me absolutely no good whatsoever.

As I walk on the treadmill, having accomplished my physical analysis, I begin the second phase of my morning therapy: maintaining that my positive attitude and mental health is in check. It is primarily about gratitude— giving thanks to the universe. My thoughts are very reflective and I use the time to make affirmations for what I am thankful for. I believe this is especially important for fostering a positive attitude. I not only give thanks for all the blessings I have, like my family, my business, and my present health (yes, even with Parkinson's it's still very much about what you have), but I also give thanks for blessings yet to come. Dwelling on the negative, like things that you don't have, can only send you into a spiral.

Remember, my whole approach and belief system revolves around the Law of Attraction: thoughts are energy, and the energy that I send out brings back more of the same. Likewise, giving thanks for blessings yet to come creates an expectation in your mind for your future. You're affirming that your future will be blessed. Feeling positive about your future, you live each day with a better attitude.

The final phase of my morning therapy is my opportunity to energizing myself through meditation. It's how I bring everything together like a chemical reaction.

Like my soul itself, my spirituality is constantly evolving and I am always learning. I certainly don't have all the answers about my spirituality—I only know what feels right in my heart, my mind and my gut. I have to trust my intuition.

There are a few personal core beliefs that I try to remind myself of that I believe influence and promote my positive attitude:

- Life's events are experiences, neither good nor bad, but rather an opportunity to learn and grow. Everything happens for a reason. I learn through pain, mistakes and failures, as well as through happiness and success.
- It is not my purpose to judge another, but only to judge myself. Everyone is on their own path. I need to practice tolerance.
- Try to always make choices first from a place of love. Listen to my heart.
- We all are connected. Everyone holds the potential of a gift—they for me, and me for them.
- We are all energy. The thoughts and attitude I send out, reflect what I receive (the Law of Attraction).
- I create my reality through my thoughts, my ideas and my beliefs.
- Be thankful.
- Love unconditionally.
- Everything is as it should be.

Those are just a few of the spiritual reminders I go over in my head as I walk on my treadmill each day. They represent some of the answers I have for myself. Which brings me back to the original question and my purpose of undertaking all this personal therapy. That is, where do I think my positive outlook comes from?

There's really only one answer I've been able to come up with. It comes from *choice*—how I choose to look at life.

That's all I know.

Oh! Except for one other thing. Baby gherkins are $1.78 a pound.

CHAPTER 39

HOW MICHAEL J. FOX CURED
PARKINSON'S DISEASE

I can't tell you how much I have labored over writing this chapter.

On the one hand, the headline screams a misleading notion to the hopes of the four-million-plus Parkinson's patients in the world, of which I am one. It is a combination of words that have such deep and emotional meaning to so many who have battled so hard. Of course, these are the words we all hope to read one day, whether they are actually attributed to Michael J. Fox, or a researcher, scientist, doctor or someone yet to be.

A cure.

So I realize that any mention of it should not be taken lightly. On the other hand, it had to be written, and Michael most definitely deserves our thanks, because the words are true.

No, I'm not about to write a fantasy sequel to one of Michael's popular *Back To The Future* movies where Marty and Doc fire up the DeLorean and travel to some distant year and find the cure for Parkinson's (although if I were a betting man, I would place all my money on Michael and his Foundation being an integral part of the cure). However, it is going to tell you about a cure that is most definitely real, nonetheless.

By this point, you've probably noticed that I use wordplay quite often in the context of my writing. I love to examine the unique meanings that words can take on, or the message they can convey through a double entendre

I especially enjoy creating thought-provoking or clever headlines and titles. Take Chapter 26, for instance, where "constant patience" was used to describe a very common symptom associated with Parkinson's disease (constipation) that, for many, has just been too uncomfortable of a topic to discuss. My solution was to create words that were both friendly and humorous, yet managed to convey the essence of the problem.

Throughout the years in my profession as an advertising creative, I've learned the importance and the art of crafting words. An attention-grabbing headline can be critical to the success of a project.

But this chapter's headline is crafted to be both engaging as well as honest. I have so much respect for Michael J. Fox and all of his dedication and hard work on behalf of Parkinson's patients, that I couldn't imagine writing anything about Michael or his foundation that ultimately was not true.

I was studying the words "Parkinson's disease" and an interesting thought suddenly occurred to me. There is a very unique meaning in the words that already existed in the very nature of the words. It simply took a creative way of looking at them to recognize it. It came to me as I thought about how we define words and how words obtain their origins. Let me take a brief moment to explain my rationale and process by which I was able to see the unique wordplay and thereby concluded that Michael had indeed provided a cure.

As an example, let's look at the word *advantage*. One definition of advantage is "a favorable circumstance which increases the chance of success"; whereas the opposite of advantage, *disadvantage*, would be "an unfavorable circumstance which decreases the chance of success.

Likewise, *comfort* refers to "a feeling of contentment with something, someone or yourself", and the opposite, *discomfort,* refers to "a.lack of contentment".

But the word *comfort* can also be defined as "a state of ease". If someone is comfortable with who they are and can portray that comfort to others, they are often said to be *at ease* with themselves. So following this train of thought, it would only be fair to say that someone who is *uncomfortable* with who they are could be referred to as being "in a state of dis-ease".

And with that definition there existed a second way of looking at the words "Parkinson's disease." Not only do the words identify a medical condition that dramatically affects the lives of millions of patients worldwide, but the same words can also describe the psychological distress experienced by PD patients and the general population alike. This *dis-ease* with Parkinson's has existed since its first classification in 1817.

For close to two hundred years, there has been a tremendous social stigma associated with Parkinson's that patients have had to cope with. The tremor, slowness of movement, shuffling of feet, and blank "mask-like" facial expression, are all characteristic symptoms of Parkinson's that have elicited feelings of shame or embarrassment from patients, as well as stares and ridicule from the general public. A great deal of this was due to lack of knowledge, understanding and awareness. The general public simply had an inability to understand the disease. More importantly, society was ignorant of the qualities, capabilities and character of people affected by Parkinson's. In short, it put everyone in a state of *dis-ease* with Parkinson's.

Then along came Michael J. Fox. More than any other person, he has almost single-handedly changed the face of Parkinson's by altering the world's comfort level with PD. He has cured the *dis-ease*. And for that, I am grateful.

It wasn't accomplished through years of intensive research, clinical trials or experimental drug therapies, and it wasn't with the development of a vaccine. There wasn't the isolation of a mutated gene or the discovery of a biomarker, and it didn't require hundreds of millions of dollars in funding. The method Michael employed was the simplest of all.

He got involved.

Michael could very easily have chosen the route of seclusion and kept his Parkinson's from the public eye; but he didn't. He listened to that voice in his head that we all hear from time to time, that intuitive voice that tells you when something is right for you to do. He got involved. It was Michael being himself.

No, better yet, it was Michael being *us*. Michael became the face for every person who struggles with the physical, emotional and the day-to-day effects of Parkinson's disease. He gave us a voice. He gave us an identity.

While there is no doubt that Michael's celebrity status played an important role in achieving this "cure", I honestly don't think there could have been a better celebrity to take on this role—because Michael wears "celebrity" far differently than most.

Unlike many celebrities, most people can identify with Michael J. Fox. He's the guy you went to high school with. He's that old friend that you've always wanted the best for. He's just so *relatable*. So when Michael shared with the world that he had Parkinson's disease, we wanted the best for him then, too.

Michael is just a very likable guy.

And so people took notice and people listened. Michael reshaped our impressions of individuals with Parkinson's disease and Parkinson's itself by dramatically increasing awareness. He became an advocate by testifying before a congressional panel about the need for greater federal funding for PD research. He brought together a world-class team of administrators, researchers and doctors to create the Michael J. Fox Foundation, which provides an avenue for Parkinson's education, support and involvement through fundraising opportunities and clinical trials. He has maintained a strong presence in the media through talk show appearances and magazine interviews to keep, in the forefront, a continuing dialogue on the work that still needs to be done. He has written books that exemplify his remarkable spirit, outlook and energy for life. All of these things speak loudly on behalf of patients as to what PD is about and, more importantly, who Parkinson's patients are and what they can accomplish.

Not unlike his role as Marty in *Back To The Future*, Michael has changed the present by making the choice to get involved. He's cured our *dis-ease* with Parkinson's and has laid the groundwork for a promising future. *Thank you.*

CHAPTER 40

DOES A BODY GOOD

I've always taken pride in being a really good cook. Whether it's tackling a recipe out of *Bon Appétit*, crafting my own version of "The Perfect Hamburger" (which I have mastered) or simply creating a recipe from scratch, I'm definitely at home in the kitchen.

Like most men, my opportunity to really shine comes on weekend mornings cooking breakfast. How do you want your eggs—over easy? Over medium? Spit grease in their face? Do you prefer an omelette, pancakes, waffles, bacon? You name it—I can make it.

Yep, I've always been comfortable in the kitchen—until one Saturday morning, a few months back.

Now on weekend mornings in our house, there's no telling what time any of my kids will awaken. At any time between 10am and 1pm, any one of them could grace us with their "sunny" morning disposition. However, just like the golden arches, I stop serving breakfast at 10:30—so if you're not up by then, you're on your own.

Quite often, however, the aroma of fresh bacon wafting through the house is enough to act like an ammonia inhalant on one of them, and on this particular morning, it did the trick on my son.

As I stood at the stove, laying a few fresh strips of bacon into the pan, Adam entered the kitchen. With barely a "Good morning," he made his way directly to the refrigerator where he retrieved a gallon of milk and began to unscrew the cap. My eyes were focused intently on my son, because my first thought was, *he's going to drink straight out of the carton!*

But he didn't. He proceeded to the cabinet, grabbed the largest glass he could find and filled it to the brim with milk. After placing the carton down, he picked up the glass and, in one continuous motion, gulped down the entire glass.

It was what I *thought* I heard next that has left an indelible scar on my brain. In fact, it makes my comfort level in the kitchen, let alone with milk, something I fear I may never quite recover from.

As my son put the glass down on the counter, like a cowboy finishing his whiskey in some bad spaghetti western, he wiped the milk mustache away from his lips, smiled at me and said, "Ahhhh!!! Nothing like an ice-cold, refreshing glass of cow's semen!"

What??? a thousand inner voices screamed in unison. *What did I just hear my son say? Did he just say "Cow's semen?" Noooo. No, no, no, that's impossible. Wait, he couldn't possibly be thinking that's what milk is, could he? That's ridiculous. He's got to be messing with me. Yeah, that's it. He's becoming a practical joker, just like his dad. Good one, Son,* I thought to myself.

But he's standing there looking at me with that grin and I just have to know if my ears were deceiving me. So with the most notably uncomfortable, half-hearted laugh and nervous quiver in my voice I asked, "Ha, ha, ummm, Son, what did you just say?"

Like most teenagers, he innocently replied, "What?"

So I repeated (against my better judgment), "Uh, ha, ha, I could swear I just heard you say, 'Nothing like an ice-cold, refreshing glass of cow's semen!'"

My son stared at me for what seemed like an eternity, before eventually bursting out laughing and saying, "Geez, Dad! Get a hearing aid already, would you. I said *cal-cium*. Nothing like an ice-cold, refreshing glass of CALCIUM."

As he walked away laughing at me, I turned around to finish the bacon, releasing two sighs of relief. One, because I had obviously misheard him, and two, because I didn't have to ask him what he thought the farmer had been doing all that time.

For a number of years now, my hearing has been on a steady decline, and the references from my family about my need for a hearing aid have been proportionally on the increase. While some of my hearing loss can be attributed to damage I inflicted on myself (such as the Ted Nugent concert back in the late seventies when our seats were right in front of the gigantic stack of speakers), the rest I can attribute to a condition called *tinnitus*.

For those unfamiliar with tinnitus, it's a condition that causes a constant ringing in your ears. Not a sweet little bell ringing like when Clarence gets his wings in *It's a Wonderful Life*; no, this is more like the high buzz of a mosquito flying close to your ear. In fact, it's like one million of the little creatures have taken refuge in your head and have learned how to use circular saws, too. It's a constant, high pitch sound that you somehow learn to live with.

To prove to my family that I was simply not hearing things and not just ignoring them, I made an appointment with an ENT (Ear, Nose and Throat doc) and had my hearing tested. Lo and behold (shortly before my Parkinson's diagnosis), I learned that I had a twenty-five percent hearing loss in both ears attributed to tinnitus, and an additional ten percent in my left ear due to Gonzo's rendition of "Cat Scratch Fever".

The most interesting information learned from the exam was that my most significant hearing loss was at high pitches— the very same pitch that happened to match my wife's voice, my daughter's voices, the dog when it whined to go out, and a baby crying because it needed a diaper change. (Okay, maybe that's a bit of an exaggeration, but women's voices are definitely harder for me to hear.)

Come to think of it, my diagnosing Parkinson's neurologist was a woman and I may very well have misunderstood her. Why, there may actually be a strong possibility that I don't have Parkinson's at all. I was under the impression she had said, "Robert, we validated your Parkinson's disease," when it's quite plausible she said, "Robert, can we validate your parking slip, please?"

That's worth checking into.

My wife and my daughters jokingly refer to my hearing loss as "selective hearing", accusing that I purposely tune them out. While there is no truth to their theory, whatsoever, as it relates to them personally, I have to admit that I *do* use selective hearing when it comes to my Parkinson's disease.

Selective hearing is my metaphor for the elements of Parkinson's that I won't allow to be part of my reality. By that I mean, I am most definitely aware of all the potentials for what Parkinson's could be for me, some of which could result in quite a negative impact on my health; but I consciously choose to tune those thoughts out and not apply the possibilities to myself.

Consequently, for some time I questioned whether I was simply in a state of denial, that perhaps I was just refusing to face the facts associated with PD. I have said before, however, when it comes to Parkinson's, there is really only one fact for me: the fact that I do have Parkinson's. That is undeniable. I have a DaTSCAN™ that shows and verifies the dopamine loss. But beyond that, I have no other facts. There isn't a doctor who can tell me with 100% certainty that my Parkinson's will absolutely be like this or absolutely be like that. No one can tell me exactly how it will impact my life. So I've chosen to say it will impact my life positively and I live my life accordingly.

So how's that working for you, Robert? you may ask.

Interestingly enough, I already have results to prove my success. Ever since my initial diagnosis with Parkinson's, there has been a reawakening of my spirituality that has given my life greater depth, clarity and balance then I have ever felt before. I honestly feel stronger with Parkinson's than I did without.

Parkinson's is not leaving me powerless. On the contrary, it is giving rise to a tremendous strength in me. While it has reminded me that I cannot control all of the outside events that occur, I *can* control how I react to them. Peace and happiness do not reside in the outside world; they reside within my heart. My own happiness is up to me.

The irony in life is that when something stands in the way of action, it actually results in causing another action. If your path in life is disrupted and you want to continue on, you have to find a way around it; that, or you stop, surrender and no longer grow.

My disruptions, my obstacles, my Parkinson's—they are all just part of life's experiences, and I will continue to find my way around them. In every life experience there is purpose, and these events promote growth, so I try to greet everything as a gift that my spirit needs.

The sounds that resonate and reverberate to the core of my very soul are positive vibrations that tell me that everything, even including my Parkinson's, is exactly as it should be. That's how I choose to hear things.

Now if only I could hear my wife with the same level of clarity.

I think she just yelled for me to come move the car.

Or was that to milk the cow?

CHAPTER 41

MASTER PEACE

In his 1889 essay, *The Decay of Lying*, Oscar Wilde "light-heartedly" suggests, "Life imitates art far more than art imitates life." Wilde's premise was that art creates the realities by which we perceive life. What is found in life and nature is not what is really there, but is really only what artists have taught people to find there, through art. As an example, Wilde cited that although there has been fog in London for centuries, one only notices the beauty and wonder of the fog because "poets and painters have taught the loveliness of such effects...they did not exist till art had invented them."

Mr. Wilde's perspective, although meant more tongue-in-cheek, suggests that the beauty and wonder of life only exists because of the creative efforts of the artist. Both life and art not only have their beginnings as a blank canvas, but without intervention, they would forever remain blank.

One might think that an artist like myself would appreciate a viewpoint such as Oscar Wilde's. I actually do find it to be a very interesting perspective. We do tend to think of both a blank canvas and a newborn child as representative of a new beginning, void of mistakes, errors or erasures where we see infinite possibilities and potential, but unlike Wilde's perspective, I see the canvas and our souls quite differently. I see the richness and beauty of a masterpiece that already exists in the very fabric of the canvas and the soul of every individual, and that each is merely awaiting the application of life and all its richness of color. Every soul is already perfect at birth, as is each blank canvas.

The stretching of the canvas and its adherence to the frame defines its potential. Likewise with the birth of a child, an infinite potential exists in each and every soul to ultimately enhance the world. It becomes more a matter of how the paint is applied to the canvas, how it is received and reflected, just as it is for how our souls experience life and reflect who we are.

For the painter, the canvas does not start blank, but rather, starts complete. It is already perfect in composition, tone, highlight and shadow because, in the mind of the artist, the art already exists. The brush will simply unveil what has always been.

Quite similarly, one could say that a newborn equally starts life complete. By its very nature, it is perfect in composition, tone, highlight and shadow because the soul was the vision of the artist, it's Creator: God. So for the baby—that ultimately matures to an adult—it is the application of life, how it is received, and the quality by which it is reflected back out to the world, which determines whether it is to be revered, cherished and admired as a work of art.

True to Oscar Wilde's perspective that life imitates art, when it comes to realizing and appreciating the beauty of our own souls, we are the painters of our own canvases. We alone determine the colors of life that we wear and reflect back to the world, by the choices we make and each encounter we experience. The people that come into our lives and all the lives that we touch, add a rainbow of color, richness and vibrancy.

To allow yourself to see and cherish the canvas of your soul as perfect, is to love yourself completely. When you can hold that vision of yourself, then you can truly reflect your brilliance to the world and master peace.

CHAPTER 42

PARK'S AND RECREATION

As I sit here soaking and relaxing with my thoughts in one of our two, matching, side-by-side, Victorian-style bathtubs, as the sun sets off in the distance, it suddenly occurred to me that there is still another topic that Parkinson's impacts that I have yet to talk about, and that is...sex.

Now, because I don't ask her to proofread anything I write, I can imagine how my wife just cringed reading that word coming from me in the context of this public forum where I have been anything but shy about sharing my most personal stories. I can hear the voice in her head, as she says to herself, *Oh no! Please tell me you're not going to talk about our sex life!*

Not to worry, Dear. When it comes to our sex life, I've got that well in hand.

This is also probably the point where my mom and my three children, who have been long-time supporters of my writing, drop off my lists of readers as well. Which would be ironic in that I learned the facts about sex from talking to my mom as a young child and then, in turn, explained the entire process to my children.

I guess you could say sex in my family is like a cookie recipe passed down from one generation to the next. Just like any good recipe—strike that, any *great* recipe—it's important that you never leave out any of the key ingredients.

Take, for example, my explanation of making a baby to my son who, if I recall correctly, was probably around seven or eight years of age at the time. For a solid thirty minutes, like Julia Childs teaching how to make Beef Bourguignon, I had done my best to explain, with vivid detail, the recipe for how a man and a woman together create the wonder of life. As I sat back proudly, as any father would, after having successfully navigated my way around the kitchen and explained the proper use of all the utensils, my son brought to my attention the omission of one key detail.

"But, Dad, how do the sperm get *through the underwear*?"

Details. Sex is definitely about the details. So please keep the above story in mind as you weigh the following observations I have made about Parkinson's disease and sex.

If putting together a tasty recipe for sex and the Parkinson's patient, one first needs to examine how the key ingredients normally combine. According to the National Parkinson Foundation, Parkinson's, by its very nature, affects the autonomic nervous system, and therefore can impact sexual performance. A *movement* disorder, by its very definition, is going to impact the routine *moves* involved in a sexual encounter.

But shouldn't that be a good thing? I always thought one popular idea behind having a healthy sexual relationship under any circumstance, was in keeping it from becoming anything but *routine*? Seems to me that using Parkinson's in a creative way could be just the thing to shake things up in the bedroom.

Let's look at the four main symptoms of PD, also called the motor symptoms:

Tremor? Sounds like a good excuse to try being tied down—but please consult your doctor first before trying anything new.

Maybe *bradykinesia* (slowness of movement) is what you're into? I honestly don't know too many people who would complain about a partner taking their time—just put on Barry White first.

Postural instability or impaired balance? Look into purchasing a waterbed— then everyone's on an even playing surface.

Rigidity. Really? Enough said.

Need a few other creative solutions?

Silk sheets or silk pajamas are recommended for reducing friction and making movement in bed easier. (CAUTION: Do not do both at the same time. I sneezed once in bed and shot myself across the room.)

With role-play, taking turns with who's in control can make the moment exciting—let your spouse hold the TV remote once in awhile.

The bottom line is try to smile. Let yourself laugh. Your good humor with how you choose to look at every situation is another great example of the positive attitude you can bring into your life.

If a simple change in attitude doesn't do the trick, then Dr. Patrick McNamara, PhD, recommends the following more conventional approaches:

- Identify root causes of the problem. If it is related to depression, treat the depression. If it is related to a reduction in sex hormones, ask your doctor about hormone replacement therapy—and so forth.
- Sometimes the root problem is the dose of PD medication you are on. Consult with your PD doctor about adjusting the dose.
- Engage in vigorous exercise whenever you can, as it will improve physical stamina and mobility. It will also enhance hormone levels in some people.
- Participate in a series of physical therapy treatments, as these can improve mobility.
- Cognitive-behavioral therapy and psychotherapy may help you work though your worries, fears and feelings of loss. Getting beyond these negative feelings may allow you to more fully enjoy the moment with your partner.
- You and your partner might consider taking a massage class together to find new ways to maintain intimacy while you are struggling with sexual dysfunction.
- Talking with your partner about what you are going through is usually a good idea, as well.

If you're like me, you'll heed the advice outlined at the Michael J. Fox Foundation website, which ended its article on Sexual Health and Parkinson's with the following recommendation: "It always helps to keep your sense of humor!"

Goodness knows, it's worked for me.

CHAPTER 43

MY LIFE IN BRACKETS

"In the event of a loss in cabin pressure, oxygen masks will deploy from overhead. Place the mask over your nose and mouth, adjust the straps for a snug fit and breathe normally".

Breathe normally? Did the flight attendant just say, "Breathe normally"? Oh yeah, that's exactly what I'll be doing if there's a loss in cabin pressure and the aircraft is plummeting from thirty thousand feet towards the earth in a downward spiral. Breathing normally.

For the moment, however, we're sitting safely on the tarmac at O'Hare International Airport, preparing for our departure to Dallas/Fort Worth. Once in Dallas, we will rent a car and make a short trek to Arlington, Texas where we'll be attending the NCAA Final Four basketball tournament—the culmination of an absolutely insane college basketball season, which saw more upsets than a full season of *The Jerry Springer Show*.

For those of you who may not follow college basketball, the NCAA college basketball tournament consists of every team in the nation *except* for the University of Illinois, pairing off in a three-week regional competition, to ultimately crown one team as the national champion. Those pairings of teams are organized into a bracket, which is subdivided into four regions of the country: South, East, West and Midwest. Within each region, sixteen teams are ranked from number one to number sixteen, which represents their overall strength or likelihood of advancing on from round to round. Theoretically, the number-one-positioned team in each region should advance the farthest in the competition and remain in the Final Four at the end of each region's competition.

Before the tournament actually begins, diehard college basketball fans fill out a personal bracket showcasing their best guestimate as to how they see all the teams advancing. It's sort of an opportunity for a Nostradamus-wanna-be to prove they really have no clairvoyance whatsoever.

So how did the 2014 tournament turn out so far?

Drop the oxygen masks and take care of yourself before helping the elderly and small children.

Tournament brackets across the nation were ripped to shreds. One corporation's "Billion-Dollar Bracket Challenge", which would pay anyone who could manage to pick an absolutely perfect bracket one billion dollars, never even had to break a sweat over the thought that they might have to pay out.

Three of the four number one seeds were eliminated in some incredible upsets, where lower-ranked teams surprised even the best analysts. As a result, number one Florida out of the South region will be squaring off against number seven Connecticut out of the East. Number two Wisconsin, representing the best of the West region, is taking on number eight Kentucky from the Midwest. From those two games will come the semi-final game, which will all lead to the determination of the national champion.

In basketball there can only be one winner.

So why is it so hard to actually pick a perfect bracket or, for that matter, even pick the Final Four? I suppose the primary reason is because we have no way of measuring the intangibles: the character, the heart and the attitude that is brought to each game on any given day by the individual players and by the team as a whole. Why, with the right amount of heart, character, determination and attitude, any competitor could put up such a fierce offense and incredible defense that they could be all but impossible to defeat.

It's those who don't give it their all, those who get complacent, and those who just assume themselves invincible, that find themselves ultimately in defeat.

It can play out much the same way in life.

Our lives are not foreign to competition. Parents compare babies, bragging that they learn faster and have achieved more than their friend's children. Kids not only compete in athletics at an early age, but, in addition, they compete for academic excellence, with an eye on college and beyond. As adults, we compete for jobs, income, physical health, beauty and love.

With that competition comes experience and, often times, success. We can become successful in love and our relationships with family, friends and business, creating a strong region of *community* in our lives. We can achieve a greater sense of physical well being by concentrating on diet and exercise, which reinforces our region of *health*. Through the sacred traditions we employ, we derive a solid region of *spirituality* or *religion*. And finally, in the fourth region we may find comfort in the strength of our *wealth*.

All in all, your life's bracket may look pretty good.

Not unlike the college tournament, however, an individual's life can also include a number of unforeseen upsets, those times when less-anticipated events like divorce, job loss, economic hardship or the diagnosis of a chronic disease such as Parkinson's can occur, to disrupt what was originally considered a very smooth path to "victory".

Those upsets don't have to be game changers. Remember that, with the right amount of heart, character, determination and attitude, any competitor can put up such a fierce offense and incredible defense, they can be all but impossible to beat.

So that's just what I've done. I've assembled a team of seven-footers with the most incredible attitude, heart and character to not only defeat Parkinson's, but I will gladly put them up against anything life wants to bring to the big game. I've seen what the other teams can throw against me and I've made my adjustments at the half. Now I'm confident I have life's game well in hand.

In contrast to the NCAA Final Four I will be attending tomorrow, the road to the finals doesn't end for me here. I'm just getting started on my life's path. I'm looking forward to every new competition and I'm progressing further towards my life's ultimate goal.

Never bet against heart, character and attitude. See for yourself on any Final Four weekend.

CHAPTER 44

WHAT ARE YOU AFRAID OF?

"I learned that courage was not the absence of fear, but the triumph over it. The brave man is not he who does not feel afraid, but he who conquers that fear."
~Nelson Mandela

Growing up, as the younger of two children, there was very little I was capable of doing that my older brother could not. After all, he was four years older which meant he was far bigger, stronger and more experienced. While as adults in our fifties the age disparity is indiscernible (though I am far better-looking and more modest), at the ages of six and ten, the differences were most definitely measurable.

Being much taller, my brother had the enviable ability to pass the forty-eight-inch height requirement that allowed him to ride the roller coasters at local amusement parks, while I was usually banished to the crazy excitement of a pink pony on the carousel. He was also, of course, first to master riding a two-wheeler, which earned him a Schwinn Sting-Ray muscle bike with the banana seat and monkey handlebars, while I was banging my knees on the dashboard of my metal AMF Fire Chief No. 503 pedal car.

So you can imagine my pride, as the "baby" of the family, in knowing there was something I could do that he couldn't. What was the talent that had my brother at a six-year-old's mercy? I could walk the full length of an unlit hallway in our house, unescorted, for the unheard of distance of fifty-feet, to turn on the light in our bedroom. Walk, mind you—not run.

That's right. My older brother was afraid of the dark.

Every night when my parents would tell us to go to bed, my brother would turn to me and say, "Come on Bob, let's go to bed," and then proceed to either push me ahead of him down the hall or outright ask me to go first and turn on the light for him. And I did it. I did it every time. I took incredible pride in being able to do that one small thing because it gave me such a sense of accomplishment to do something that he could not.

But here's the funny part. I was afraid, too.

Unbeknownst to my brother, I was as equally afraid of the dark, but rather than letting it paralyze me, I turned it into a personal challenge for myself. You see, as much as I feared going down that hall, I repeatedly kept telling myself that if I could do this one thing, that I would not only have something I could do that my brother could not, but maybe he might have a new level of respect for me—that he might look up to me even though I was much smaller. I had given myself a purpose for overcoming my fears.

It took more than just having a goal to succeed at my challenge. It took some strategy and creative thought as well.

In addition to my thoughts about the possible outcome, I also kept a very strong focus on the fact that I was not alone. After all, my parents were in the house and my brother was just a few steps behind me, as I continued with purpose down the hall (my eyes closed for most of the way, as well).

Every time, I ultimately succeeded in navigating my way through the darkness to find the light. Over time it not only became easier for me, but it eventually became easier for my brother, too, until he finally realized he didn't need me to lead the way anymore—he had the confidence to do it himself.

I find it very interesting that a fear of the dark is one of the earliest and most common childhood fears. It is understandably frightening to a child's developing mind. At that early age, we crave security, safety and comfort in a world we are just coming to know. The darkness represents the unknown, the things we cannot see. And when we do not have anything real or tangible to see, we are left with only our imagination, and for some reason we imagine the worst. We imagine monsters, demons and boogeymen.

But are they there? No. Our imagination creates our own fears. In essence, we are left to learn how to overcome our own imaginations. We can choose to imagine the worst, or we can choose to imagine the best.

Courage, to me, is the strength to imagine something better in the face of your fears.

The darkness associated with the unknown is not just limited to adolescents; quite the contrary. Adults often allow fear of the unknown to limit our ability to live happy and fulfilling lives, all because we don't have the courage to imagine the existence of angels within the darkness. Instead, we give more thought to fantasies of demons, monsters and boogeymen. We're conditioned to need proof that everything will be ok, rather than being able to trust that there is good in both darkness and in light.

The expression, "seeing is believing", fortifies the notion that, until you are shown the facts or the proof of a situation, there is nothing for you to be sure of. Until the light is turned on, there is no way to know what's in store for you.

I feel the more poignant expression to be "believing is seeing," which means that we create our own reality (or things that we see in our life) by the way we choose to believe.

When I was given a diagnosis of Parkinson's disease, the lights were immediately turned off and I was plunged into total darkness. It was very much like the room I'd walk into as a child, because the darkness of Parkinson's is also filled with unknowns. I didn't know what to expect and was left with only my imagination about what could be in store for me. Will it be monsters, demons and boogeymen?

I decided early on that I wasn't going to let the diagnosis paralyze me. I chose to believe I could see a different outcome. I began to imagine that the best actually existed in this place where I could see absolutely nothing, that was completely foreign to me.

And you know what? I was afraid. I *am* afraid.

So I did the only thing I know how to do to face of my fears. I gave myself a challenge. I challenged myself to imagine goodness in the darkness. I gave myself the choice to "believe it—and I'll see it." For all these months, I've been writing, learning, discovering and, most of all, putting all my belief in a better outcome with Parkinson's. By taking on a positive attitude, I'll see positive results.

Taking this path of courage isn't something that no one else has ever done, but it's most definitely been about showing others that they can do it, too. Anyone can make the choice to be happy.

With each chapter I write, I walk down that hall again and I turn on the light. It's my way to repeatedly remind myself that there is goodness that exists in the dark. My heart, my soul and my spirit are the lights that allow me to see it.

And you know what? I'm seeing it.

I'm seeing it brighter than ever.

CHAPTER 45

IN THE SPIRIT OF
TOGETHERNESS

Every person who has come into my life has been a blessing. As a result of my experience with Parkinson's disease over the past two years, I have had the pleasure of personally meeting a number of extraordinary individuals. People who, realize it or not, have become a tremendous part of my life.

I have met doctors and clinicians at Northwestern Memorial Hospital who have dedicated their lives not only to the field of neurology, but more specifically to the study and service of finding a cure for Parkinson's disease.

I have personally come to know the efforts of agencies such as the National Parkinson Foundation and the Michael J. Fox Foundation for Parkinson's Research, whose work truly defines their names. They are the very *foundations* that support research and doctors through generating awareness, advocating for patient care, creating and supporting clinical trials and providing essential funding.

I've met Staci Page, a transformational healing therapist and spiritual guide, who helped me reawaken my spirituality, which, in turn, has helped me heal and find greater comfort and peace with Parkinson's and every facet of my life.

Through fundraising initiatives like our Party for Parkinson's, I've met business owners who give back to the community that supports them by hosting and contributing their business facilities and staff.

I've met complete strangers, community members and neighbors, whose lives have been touched in some way by Parkinson's and wanted to do something to honor a loved one, a co-worker or a friend. And finally there are people who have had no experience with Parkinson's, but because of their strong sense of humanity, want to be a part of a greater effort.

I've been blessed to have my eyes opened to witness what incredible, loving hearts my personal friends and family have, not only for me, but also for a cause that is close to my heart.

Finally, there are the wonderful individuals I have connected with through my writings about Parkinson's and spirituality. I've received emails and letters from some, and have struck up some wonderful, ongoing correspondences with a few as well—people who I have never had the pleasure of meeting face to face, but I feel connected to, just the same.

Everyone who knows me and knows about my journaling, understands that what I am doing is all about making connections. I am rediscovering my connection with my own spirituality, and, in doing so, I'm discovering how that connection plays into my positive relationship with Parkinson's. The two go hand in hand, but it also has gone well beyond that. If sharing my approach for dealing positively with Parkinson's might inspire or give hope to another patient or their loved ones—then my efforts are worthwhile.

Collectively, this has fostered an awareness that we are all connected as people, as one group of souls, and whether it's for Parkinson's, cancer, or feeding hungry children, we are all in this together. Together as one, there is no limit to what we can do or accomplish.

Over these past months of writing and soul searching, one of the biggest personal discoveries I have made is that there is a light glowing deep inside of me. The light is the spirit of love. Every time I connect with someone and see the light in them, my light grows a little brighter. I want to see that light spread to other people and help them remember the best part of themselves.

Getting involved can do that. For Parkinson's patients it's empowering. It allows you to be an active part in managing your disease. You're actually contributing to the effort to find a cure as opposed to simply waiting for it. It introduces you to a community that you are already a part of, and best of all, by getting involved, the life you end up changing may just be your own.

CHAPTER 46

A LOVE LETTER

My personal belief is that each of us walks a unique path in life—a path that we actually chose for ourselves. Our spirit designed it out of necessity for growth and evolution. What is truly remarkable about each and every path is, there is no way of knowing what or who might appear around the next turn or over the horizon of tomorrow. Yet the answers are there, as sure as the sun will rise with them. Our spiritual self knows, but our human form does not. It accepts that tomorrow's experiences are meant to be and have divine purpose for us. Everything is as it is meant to be.

However, when you do discover something or someone who changes your life, you can't help but be surprised.

I'm confident our paths had crossed many times in the past, because when we finally did meet, it was as if I had known you from every lifetime before. A wave of familiarity washed over me as if to say that I had found my way back to my best friend after having been lost. With our reintroduction, there was no longer anything to fear. I was safe and at home with you.

I don't believe you were the one seeking to find me as much as I had been looking for you. I needed you and that desire led me to you. Maybe living without you was part of a process I had to go through to appreciate all that you are to me now.

In you is reflected the best part of myself, because you challenge me to be a better person: more tolerant, patient, kind, respectful and loving—all the qualities that I know exist in you.

You have loved me with all of your heart, void of demands or expectations, and you never lost your belief in everything about me. You've seen me at my worst when my faults are worn like tattered clothing for all to see, and still you find it in your heart to forgive me. You have always accepted me for who I am.

You've supported me with your love and held me in your embrace when my life's challenges have been their greatest. You've shown me that together there is nothing we cannot overcome. With every great accomplishment I've made, you've quietly acknowledged how pleased you were with me. Nothing I have achieved has ever come as a surprise to you, because you have always loved me and believed in me from the start.

We are so much a part of each other that, at times, I lose my sense of where one of us starts and the other begins. With you, it's as if love melts all separate being into one. There is no other but the sum of us together. You taught me that the mate for my soul was not to be found in one, but rather in the love of all. That is where my soul would be complete.

You share a vision of a world where there is no pain, no anger or hurt because you see the perfection that exists in everyone, just as it exists in every flower that grows in a field.

I realize that I don't do enough to express how much I love you, yet your love for me never wavers. What I see as a small gesture on my part, you receive on the grandest of scales. It is by your own example that I have come to learn that, the best way to love you in return, is to love everyone as you love me—for the greatest compliment of your love is to emulate you and share it with the world.

As I've walked my path in life, there have been far too many times that I've lost sight of you and felt I was alone. I came to learn that it's because I was looking too far ahead. The human part of me was looking too far over the horizon, while my spirit knew you were with me all along. You were inside me—in my heart and in my soul—and I never had been alone.

And I never will be again.

I love you.

CHAPTER 47

CONNECTING THE DOTS

As a small child, I vividly remember sitting in the waiting room of my pediatrician's office with a *Highlights* magazine in my lap. *Highlights* was a children's magazine that somehow made me feel better regardless of how sick I was. Thumbing through the pages of puzzles, riddles, word games and stories, I considered myself incredibly lucky if I happened to be the first child to open that particular issue. That meant that no other child had penciled in the solutions. The answers were yours and yours alone to find.

I had two favorite games in *Highlights* magazine. The first was "What's Different Here?" which depicted two nearly identical drawings, where the object was to find as many of the dissimilarities as possible and circle them. The other game was "Connect the Dots." I loved the process of meticulously working my way from one letter to the next, coupled with the anticipation of unveiling the image that my lines would create in the end. The magazine usually provided a vague teaser that gave a hint as to what the image would be, but for me, going from A to B and B to C and so on, to ultimately reveal the big picture at the end, was mesmerizing and would completely occupy my time until the doctor was ready to see me.

A great deal of my writing has offered glimpses into my childhood that I felt either had a direct correlation to shaping my positive attitude towards life and Parkinson's disease, or they served as metaphors for explaining my perspective. As my journaling continues to shed more light on that attitude, there's one recurrent theme, no matter what my age.

Connections. They have played such an important role in my life.

We start our lives connected, as a baby in the womb, literally tethered to our mothers by an umbilical chord.

Eventually we make the transition from the nurturing embrace of our mother's arms, which offer safety and comfort, to being put down (disconnected) to crawl and enter our own little world. It's very symbolic of leaving the nest. From that point on, we're exposed to the inevitability of injuries: physically, emotionally, and spiritually.

Life is rough. Life is fragile. It's part of developing our separate self. But we're not meant to go through life alone. We're all really in this together. We strive to maintain connections and we endeavor to make new ones. I honestly think that, without connections, we're lost. Our connections are meant to assist us, guide us and help us find our way. Our connections ultimately reveal life's big picture.

Early on as a parent I made a vow to always try to remember what it was like to be my children's ages. It was one of my conscious efforts to stay connected to my children by remaining connected to my own childhood.

So often we hear of kids saying, "My parent's just don't get me. They have no clue what my life is about."

Well, I was determined to never hear that. As a result, I took notice very early on of my children's regular question, "What was it like when you were a kid, Dad?" That desire to know that their struggles and anxieties were not unique was not only their way of establishing a sense of security for themselves, but also an opportunity for me to reinforce another connection between us. I loved sharing my stories with my children. It helped them and it helped me. And I realize that, even now, I am continuing to tell them my stories.

As they slowly matured, however, the questions became fewer and farther between, and the need on my part to maintain those connections became greater and greater. But I had the sense to anticipate that coming, because I remembered being their age. I knew the sixteen- and seventeen-year-old phase would one day be here and I would suddenly become the father who, in their eyes, hadn't a clue.

So I had a plan—and for any parents who still have young children, I highly recommend this plan.

Around the time my third child, Adam, was six years of age, I began talking about three trips I wanted to take, one with each of my children. Each was going to be a very special trip. Year after year I reminded them about the trip that was to come. The plan was to take each of my children on a trip of their own when they turned sixteen, just the two of us for four to five days, anywhere of their choosing within the United States. I presented it as my way of celebrating their birthday—a milestone in their life. I explained that in choosing a destination, they ought to think about what is important to them. For me, of course, it was simply going to be an opportunity to reconnect with my teenager who, at that future time, might just be thinking their dad is completely out of touch.

When my oldest daughter Amanda turned sixteen, her love at the time was dancing. Like most sixteen-year-old girls, shopping fit into her interests as well. Amanda was my sophisticated child with an "old soul", even as a young girl. When other children were craving macaroni and cheese, Amanda was sampling steamed artichokes. When presented with a choice of cookies and cake for dessert, Amanda would usually opt for an apple or an orange. Additionally, as a young girl she exhibited a confidence and poise about her, and she loved organizing her siblings for living room matinee dance recitals on Sunday mornings. (Very fittingly, she is now an elementary education schoolteacher.) So it wasn't surprising to me that Amanda's destination of choice for our special father-daughter trip was New York City.

Now at the point of Amanda's decision to go to the Big Apple, what had all along been planned as a dad and daughter trip was suddenly changing it's dynamic. Either my wife simply couldn't bear the thought of just Amanda and I going to New York City with all of that shopping to be done, or Amanda couldn't imagine her father being willing to do that much shopping; regardless, it soon became the three of us instead of the original two. My only stipulation was that my wife had to agree that no matter where our other two children chose to go on their trips, she would attend those as well.

Agreed.

I made arrangements for us to stay at the Waldorf Astoria. We went to see Mary Poppins on Broadway, attended the New York City ballet, went shopping and sight seeing, and had some of the most magnificent food—from breakfast at Balthazar's, to dinner at The Modern in the Museum of Modern Art. We stood on the top of the Empire State Building and, as Amanda's father, I stood on top of the world. She was discovering a city she had never seen, while I was discovering the woman my daughter was becoming. The trip was everything I had hoped for.

Erica, my youngest daughter is my free spirit. In her life, she hears the beat of a different drum. She would probably be surprised to hear me say this, but she is the one of my three children that reminds me the most of myself. She is incredibly strong-willed, independent and compassionate. She is my empathic child and, from a very early age, has always been the one who has never shied away from standing up for the underdog or stating her views when she feels something is wrong. Her independent nature and desire to fly free was apparent early on, in that she didn't like to be held or hugged—it was too confining for her. She was very loving and affectionate, but Erica wanted to be free to run like the wind—which might explain why she became fascinated with horses and grew up taking riding lessons.

Erica's choice for her trip? Greenough, Montana and the Paws Up Ranch and Resort, nestled in the Blackfoot Valley near Glacier National Park. There we enjoyed five days of camping and beauty beyond belief. In a setting where they filmed the movie *A River Runs Through It* with Brad Pitt, we fly fished, hiked, road horses and ATVs, and rappelled. Instead of navigating the rivers of concrete and steel in New York City, we were white water rafting and traversing the obstacles of the Blackfoot River. It was during this latter event that I found myself becoming closer to Erica than ever before.

As we were getting ready to set off on our rafting adventure, we were given the choice of riding in a large raft that held around twelve individuals and a professional guide, or in our own kayak, just the two of us.

No experience and no skill? That's sounded perfect for Erica and I.

My wife chose the safer and saner route, riding in the big raft that was professionally manned by an Abercrombie & Fitch model who used his abdominal muscles to steer the raft.

As we took to the water and paddled away from shore, navigation was easy enough. It was a quiet and peaceful river that ran between cavernous mountain walls. The water was so still that it was almost effortless to keep the kayak moving. Erica and I chatted and laughed together, and we were really enjoying the pace. Suddenly, we could see that was all about to change. Around a bend, the glass-like surface of the water was replaced with a churning river, dotted with boulders. It looked like someone had meticulously created an obstacle course for us to maneuver. We both sat up with excitement and readied ourselves for what would lie ahead.

As we entered the rapids, Erica and I began to discover an unspoken rhythm with the oars. She in the front and myself steering in the rear of the kayak, we found ourselves doing well rather quickly. We were intensely focused on the task at hand, as Erica would call out boulders that lay ahead for me to steer us clear of. It actually seemed as though we were going to successfully navigate this liquid Pachinko machine and come out the other side of it unscathed. But like Chicago weather in March, the waters of the Blackfoot River can quickly change.

Have you ever observed a car accident on the side of the road where there is ample open space all around the scene, yet the car inevitably is wrapped around a light pole or a tree? Or how many golfers have had a tree ahead of them that partially obscures a clear shot to the green; a tree that, for all intents and purposes, is seventy percent air, but nonetheless manages to make contact with a tiny sphere the size of...well, a golf ball? There seems to be an unwritten law of nature that says the harder you try to avoid an object, the greater the chance you will come in contact with it—and Erica and I were about to prove it.

Directly ahead, slightly right of center in the river was a large boulder. I knew exactly where it was because Erica kept barking out its position to me like she was the lookout on the deck of the Titanic. The harder she and I paddled the kayak to try and steer clear of it, the more determined the boulder was to make contact with us. Honestly, if I didn't know better, I would have sworn the boulder just got up and ran out in front of us.

As our kayak eventually made contact with the rock, it slid the bow of our boat to the left, turning us sideways, which dramatically increased our surface area for the raging waters to push harder against. The kayak was quickly lodged firmly against this massive stone. The incredible force of the river was more than we were able to control. We were locked in place. As I tried to push us free using my oar, we slowly began to list backwards, causing Erica to panic and shift her weight in an attempt to steady the boat. The move lurched the kayak violently backward, allowing water to rush in and quickly dump us, and all of our cargo, into the raging river. We found ourselves in the water separated by the boat, with Erica between the boat and the boulder. To make matters worse, the strong undercurrent was slowly pulling Erica's feet under the rock.

And then it happened.

My sixteen-year-old daughter looked at me with more fear in her panic-filled eyes than I had ever seen before. Sensing she was about to be swept down the river or, worse yet, pulled under the boulder, Erica reached out to me with both arms and screamed, "Dad! Please don't let me go!" In that moment, that fraction of a second, in a mere blink of an eye, the clock turned back twelve years to the little four-year-old girl that I always wanted so badly to hold and hug. And here she was now, reaching out and asking me to hold onto her.

There was absolutely no way I would let her go.

Pushing aside the kayak that separated us, I watched as the current quickly grabbed hold of the boat and oars and pulled them into the open current. But as rapidly as the river had our boat, I had Erica in my arms and I held on tight.

My son, Adam, made a choice for his trip that frankly, didn't surprise me. And in all honesty I couldn't have been more pleased with his decision.

Adam has a soul filled with love—overflowing with love, actually. Because of that he gives it out in abundance. I know that, in his heart, he'd love to have it reciprocated in the same volume, but it's not. Yet that doesn't deter Adam or cause him to throttle back what he gives—no, not in the least. For example, at sixteen years of age, when some teenagers want to be anywhere but with their family, Adam will offer to go stay at his grandparents' house because he knows they appreciate the company. He understands the value of family and the true love associated with it.

For his sixteenth birthday adventure, Adam chose to return to a family vacation spot we had frequented every summer for a number of years, a cabin on a chain of lakes in the Northwoods of Wisconsin. It was a place where we would fish, boat and, best of all, come together as a family for an entire week.

Adam wanted his trip to be a reuniting of our family. He insisted that rather than taking a trip just for himself, the best way he could celebrate would be for all of us to be together. Consequently, for my sons sixteenth birthday, we rented the cabin once again and we had a fantastic time reconnecting.

The three trips accomplished exactly what I had hoped they would. They connected my children to their family at a time in their lives when there was plenty of distraction to pull them elsewhere.

Tremors in the Universe has been an examination and a sharing of the "highlights" of my journey so far. The challenge has been to discover the answers to all the puzzles and riddles that encompass my experience with Parkinson's disease and spirituality. My fascination with the "What's different?" images, most definitely mirrors my unique perspective on PD and outlook on life. Connecting the dots is precisely what I am doing in order to learn from the experiences along my life's path. I've discovered that each and every connection has importance, and that each new connection provides the opportunity for me to learn more and move further along. Although there are still plenty of dots to be connected, I am beginning to see the big picture.

Chapter 48

Attitude & Gratitude

I've been asked many times how I manage to keep such a positive attitude in the midst of my diagnosis of Parkinson's disease, to which I often respond, "I have Parkinson's disease?"

Humor is definitely one component for coping (along with denial and sheer stubbornness), but for me it really boils down to the two key elements: *attitude* and *gratitude*.

With attitude, I make a conscious choice to be happy and think positively. The alternative simply doesn't appeal to me. So I demand that my Parkinson's fit within my happiness or it has to get lost. With gratitude, I find something new to be thankful for each day. Doing both is honestly quite easy for me, so I'd like to share some tips:

- "Think" a smile. Try it. Close your eyes and picture a smile in your mind.
- Give thanks for things that are *going to come* to you. Creating an expectation in your mind that tomorrow holds a gift for you does wonders towards fostering a positive outlook.
- Never allow others to have the power over your mood. It's yours. Protect it.
- Choose to be happy, always. Happiness is a choice you can always make for yourself, regardless of your circumstances.
- Once in awhile, eat your dessert before your dinner.

- Challenges are only as difficult as you define them to be. Don't be so hard on yourself.
- Always kiss on the lips.
- Admire beauty in all its forms.
- Accept what is or accept the role of changing it.
- Remind yourself: Anything is possible.
- Meditate.
- Exercise.
- The best way to accept a compliment is with a "thank you".
- When you're imagining the worst, look up the definition of imagination.
- Laugh so hard that you cry, and cry so hard that you laugh.
- Believe that everything is as it should be.
- Make all your decisions from a place of love.
- If you're afraid of dying, give more of yourself. That way you'll insure that there's more of you that remains around.
- Get a massage.
- Show compassion, empathy and love every day.
- Make a difference in your life; then, go make a difference in the life of another.
- Picture a better world, and then learn to draw.

I was given this life, because I'm strong enough to live it. The last thing I plan to do is allow Parkinson's disease to stop me.

CHAPTER 49

MAKING CHANGE

"The purpose of life is to live it, to taste experience to the utmost, to reach out eagerly and without fear for newer and richer experience." ~Eleanor Roosevelt

The only constant in life is change. Alteration is never-ending. From the very beginning of time, our universe has been in a constant state of chaos, expanding further and further into the limitless depths of the heavens and an unknown abyss. Stars are continually born and stars continue to die. And with every second of every day, another instant in time passes us by, leaving that moment to never be repeated again. The present, which is unique unto itself, has a life span equal to only the blink of an eye.

As humans, we average 60,000 thoughts per day, yet we retain less than one percent because, as quickly as one idea or thought pops into our head, it is gone. The same holds true for the sounds that reverberate in our ears, only to be followed by silence. We satiate our sense of taste with flavors that come alive in our mouths, and seconds later, wash it away with drink. We can open our eyes to the pallet of the world, but we blink and it all disappears.

Our friends and our lovers come and go, relatives die and countless others are born. The market can be up and the market can go down and wealth will be acquired and lost. Sometimes you will succeed and sometimes you will fail. And through it all one thing remains constant: *no two moments in time will ever be the same.*

And that's ok!

It's how the universe was intended. It's fundamentally the way things are supposed to be—ever-evolving, ever-changing. Life is fluid. It's uncertain chaos.

But as humans, we tend not to do well with lack of order. We have evolved to respond in a very odd way to this natural flow and rhythm in our universe. We take a moment or event and label it good, bad or indifferent based on how it made us feel, when in essence it wasn't anything of the sort. It was merely an experience. Then, based on how we perceive the event, we respond out of habit with a predetermined mindset.

If we classified an event as a good experience, then we strive to capture that moment, hold onto it to keep it from ever slipping away. The thought of how good it was and the feelings it evoked become addictive. When the thought begins to diminish or the feelings start to slip away, then we will put all our efforts into trying to make that event happen again so as to hopefully repeat that experience that made us feel so good.

The flip side of the coin is when we give an experience the moniker of "bad". And when we label something as bad it's the same as poison. We do whatever we can to push it away, dismiss it, refute it and destroy all recollection of it. Some even have such difficulty with a bad experience that they wear it more like a permanent tattoo than a bruise that is bound to fade.

In the middle of these two powerhouse mindsets exists indifference—the vanilla, the boring, the dull, the uneventful experiences that are neither good nor bad. These are the experiences we deem unworthy of our attention. Yet, these are the experiences that make up ninety percent of our lives. Although they constitute the bulk of our existence, we prefer to focus ninety percent of our attention where the drama is— back to our seesaw battle between lust and disgust. We chase after the pleasurable experiences and flee from the negative ones, leaving this middle mindset shortchanged for our attention.

What I've come to realize since my diagnosis of Parkinson's disease is that far too much of the emphasis in my life had been on trying to figure out what was right or what was wrong, what was good and what was bad—and somehow thinking I had control over that. The truth of the matter is that the majority of what comes into my life I have absolutely no control over. It doesn't really matter whether I label it as "good" or "bad".

It just *is*. It's all exactly as it is supposed to be. It is ordered chaos.

For clarity of thought I am not referring to my moral compass, for I think it's definitely important to have a sense of right and wrong in how you live your life, especially in the context of how you treat others. No, the labeling I am referring to is our categorization of the day-to-day events that make up our lives.

I could have very easily labeled my Parkinson's diagnosis as a bad thing, but why should I? It hadn't immediately done anything to me. My life didn't instantaneously become worse from one second to the next, so why should I pigeonhole Parkinson's into a definition of my own creation as *bad*?

With so much unpredictability in life, and chaos in the uncertain world that we live in, I have learned that all of the over-analyzing, over-planning, over-thinking and over-labeling, really doesn't accomplish anything. It doesn't make me feel any better or any different by labeling it. In actuality it makes me feel worse. If I were to try to compartmentalize everything that happens to me, I would be overwhelmed by the chaos of life. The anxiety and stress I would create for myself by trying to label every event in my life, is simply lunacy. It is a trap.

By attempting to define what is "good" for myself and judge every experience against that standard, I set myself up for an incredible disappointment when events come along that don't fit that label. Likewise, when I allow myself to be engulfed by the hurt and rejection of something unpleasant, I momentarily stop moving forward. I stop experiencing the infinite choices that are afforded me during my life's journey.

Our inability to accept that which we cannot control is at the heart of what keeps so many of us from moving forward, moving past obstacles, overcoming challenges, and achieving true happiness. I can't control what happens to me. I can only control how I react.

To live a happy life, we have to learn to honestly and sincerely embrace life exactly the way it is, with the trust and belief that everything is as it should be: unpredictable, good, bad, indifferent and fantastic!

It really isn't important whether or not something is good or bad, but more importantly that we accept that life *just is*—it's there for the living, it's presenting us with experiences one after another, not for us to bog ourselves down with defining, but rather inviting us to relish in and enjoy.

Reach out eagerly. Accept that everything is as it should be. It *all* has divine purpose. Most of all stop worrying and get on with living!

CHAPTER 50

IT AIN'T OVER 'TIL IT'S OVER

"It's hard to beat a person who never gives up." ~Babe Ruth

From the time I was six years old until I was well into my forties, I loved playing organized baseball. I was never really that good at it but I did love playing the game, maybe because being in the game was far better than watching from the stands. To me, watching baseball is like watching the grass grow. Come to think of it, as an outfielder in pee wee baseball, I think I watched the grass grow there as well, because the ball rarely, if ever, got hit into the outfield.

I admit that I had a few occasions of greatness on the diamond over the years like pitching a no-hitter, making the all-star team, and being part of turning a triple play. Otherwise, I was mediocre at best. It never deterred me, however, and I continued to play year after year.

My strength in baseball was my arm. Boy, could I throw a ball. As a result, I was either delegated to outfield because I could get the ball to the infield quickly and accurately; put at third base because I had a strong enough throw to reach first base; or I was a starting pitcher. Pitching was my favorite. When I was pitching, I couldn't help but feel I was in control of the game's outcome. Eventually I came to realize that wasn't at all true. There were eight other teammates on the field and we all played an integral part in whether we won or lost.

During the entire time I played organized baseball, I always wore the number "3" on my jersey. That was Babe Ruth's number and Babe was one of the greatest home run hitters of all time. I had always hoped that since I had Babe Ruth's number, maybe I'd be able to slug a ball like him. Unfortunately, that wasn't the case.

In little league baseball, my weakness was definitely my hitting. I was a terrible hitter. Rarely did I have a batting average over two hundred, which made being a pitcher all the better. Pitchers didn't need to be good hitters because statistically they had fewer at bats—at least that's what I told everybody. Truth of the matter was, I was afraid of the ball. A hanging curve ball, especially. I just didn't want to get hit. I assumed it was going to really hurt. Babe Ruth was fearless, but my problem was fear.

My turn at bat typically went something like this. First I'd look down to the third base coach to get my sign, which was usually him scratching his nose, adjusting his hat, wiping one hand across his chest and one hand down his pants leg. *Oh wait, that's my dad in the stands eating a hot dog. "Oh, hey, Dad!"* which would be followed by my coach hollaring "Bob! Get your head in the game!"

I'd then hold one hand up to the umpire as I dug in my back foot into the batters box. (The hand was my way of stalling, indicating, "Please don't let that guy throw at me yet.") Then I'd bring my front foot into the box and take two or three practice swings while the catcher gave his signs to the pitcher and trash-talked me to get in my head, stuff like, "This guy couldn't hit a ball if his grandmother was pitching!" You know, it's bad enough that I'm afraid the guy on the mound is going to drill a fast ball into my head, but now I've got a guy behind me who's distracting me because he thinks my grandma could strike me out.

Then the pitch comes in—a hanging curve ball. It leaves the pitchers hand, heading straight for my head. Just as it gets close enough to scare the daylights out of me, the spin of the ball makes it curve and drop right into the catcher's glove for a strike. As a batter, I'm supposed to hang in there and swing. Problem was, I always baled and stepped out of the box.

"Strike one!" the umpire would yell.

"Ugh", I'd usually grunt in frustration.

"Good pitch, Grandma!" the catcher would bark as he threw the ball back to the mound, and then would look at me and laugh.

The real kicker was that it still beat watching from the stands. There was no other place I wanted to be but in the game, and there was absolutely no way I ever would have given up even with the strong possibility that I was going to strike out (which I did quite often). I still wanted to have my chance at the plate.

No matter how often I found myself walking back to the bench instead of running down to first, I always knew there would be another opportunity for me. Maybe, just *maybe* that next time, with hope, faith and determination, things might turn out differently. Why, I might even manage to hit a home run—or better yet, a grand slam that wins the game.

It could happen. After all, I wear number 3.

But it was never going to happen if I wasn't a player in that game.

I look at Parkinson's the very same way. From the very beginning, there was no question in my mind that I wanted to be an active participant in the game. I wanted a chance to compete. For me, that came in the form of signing up for clinical trials. Getting involved was getting in the game. What was the alternative? Sitting on the bench, waiting to see what Parkinson's was going to throw at me? No way. I was drafted onto this team (not my team of choice, by any means, but I'm on the roster nonetheless.) If I'm on the team, I want my chance to compete and maybe, just *maybe*, make a difference.

Sure, Parkinson's throws curve balls at me. Big, scary, hanging curve balls that always aim at my head—trying to mess with me, trying to make me bale out. The stories of what other patients have gone through are like the catcher talking trash to me. "What do you think you're going to do?"

Well, you know what? I'm going to swing. I'm no longer afraid of life's curve balls. A curve ball is a perceived illusion—it works only when you believe it can hurt you. Plant your feet solid, stand your ground and set your mind clearly on the fact that it's all about perception, and you'll quickly find yourself swinging for the fences.

The greatest thing in my game has been the results. The clinical trials are putting runners on base and we're slowly driving them in. With each run, we're chipping away at the seemingly insurmountable lead that Parkinson's has held onto for far too long. There is definitely an offensive momentum in our favor right now. We're still in the early innings and we desperately need more people to step up to the plate and register for a clinical trial.

If you're interested in becoming a part of the team and taking an active role in helping to speed the defeat of PD, the Michael J. Fox Foundation for Parkinson's Research (www.michaeljfox.org) is a great place to start. There, you will find a complete list of trials being conducted and ways to contribute.

Perhaps participating in a clinical trial isn't your thing, but you'd still like to contribute to the outcome. Well, there's a saying in baseball (one that I personally heard quite often) that says, "A walk is as good as a hit"—which basically means, get on base any way that you can. Runners on base mean potential runs.

Lucky for Parkinson's supporters, the National Parkinson's Foundation hosts the Moving Day walk in cities across the United States, making it easy to get in the game. In 2013, over 20,000 walkers participated and in my home city of Chicago, and we raised well over $350,000.

It turns out a walk can be a tremendous hit!

For more information on a Moving Day walk near you, visit: www3. parkinson.org.

The bottom line is, get involved. Whether you sign up to participate in a clinical trial, or you prefer to fundraise or donate your time or money, being in the game makes all the difference in the world. As a patient, it is not only empowering, but it can change your life.

My participation may not ultimately be the home run that wins this game, but I will know, in my heart, that I participated, I competed, and I never gave up.

CHAPTER 51
MORE TO COME

As I mentioned at the very beginning of this book, the first public sharing of my writing, thoughts and outlook regarding my life with Parkinson's and spirituality began as a blog some six months ago. Over that period of time, my loyal readers became very familiar with a sign-off I used at the conclusion of every post: *More to come.*

That sign-off was my way of signifying that there would be another post, be it the following week, two weeks later or whenever. I would say "more to come" because I wanted the readers to know there were still more words that I wanted to say, more experiences I wanted to share, more love I wanted to express and more hope I wanted to foster.

There still is, even today.

"More to come" is also my way of saying I'm not quitting; I'm not giving up—there is more of me to come.

But there is also the sad truth that another reason existed for those words at the close, and that is because, for now Parkinson's has no end in sight—and that's quite a sobering thought for me. When it comes to Parkinson's disease, for myself and for others, there is still...more to come.

When I started writing *Tremors in the Universe,* I made the decision to document my experience with Parkinson's disease in an extremely personal way. It wasn't a difficult decision for me to make—it had to be that way if I was going to help myself. And it most definitely had to be that way if I thought that it might help someone else. If I was going to ask people to read my account of living with this disease, I had to be willing to share with them an intimate side of it. Only then could I be sure I had given them something useful to relate to, or to compare with their own personal experience.

How could I help others if I couldn't help myself first?

My wife acknowledged, in the very beginning, that she wouldn't be able to do what I was doing. She wouldn't be able to share her most intimate feelings and thoughts with perfect strangers. While I understood that and respected that, as I said to her at the time, it's a lot easier for me to share the details of my life *because* it's with total strangers. It's my close, personal friends that I require the most courage to open up to.

I'm glad I made the decision to be transparent in my writing, because a very enlightening thing has transpired as a result of my opening up. What has happened is that those perfect strangers who were so easy to "talk" to, have now become friends. Through my choice to share my story, others have had the opportunity to discuss theirs. And theirs is equally as important as mine.

When I went online to research Parkinson's in an attempt to understand what to expect of this journey, I discovered a lot of clinical information outlining symptoms, treatments and prognosis, but no deeply personal accounts of what people were emotionally going through. How were they mentally reacting to it? What were they feeling outside of the symptoms of the disease itself? What were they thinking—were they scared? Were they hopeful? Or were they just ambivalent? And what methods were they employing to deal with all aspects of the disease? How were they choosing to emotionally cope?

Nothing.

I decided to write from a personal perspective that shared it all: pain, fear, hope, love and faith. Along the way, I discovered that I wasn't only finding a unique perspective for dealing with Parkinson's; I was finding a unique perspective for dealing with life.

My Parkinson's is in its early stages right now, just two and a half years since my diagnosis. I know in my heart that there is the potential for a lot more to come. My plans are to change nothing. I will write for as long as I am capable, continuing to document my experience with the disease. I will continue to fundraise and advocate for Parkinson's research, and I definitely will continue to participate in clinical trials.

Parkinson's is presently a challenge that I have been given to experience in my life. I'm not a stranger to challenges; I've had other ones before. If my Parkinson's were to be gone tomorrow, I would feel with certainty that I'd be given a new challenge in my future. I believe they offer our souls opportunity for growth and evolution.

"More to come" is also about life. It represents the challenges we all must face. If you're not being challenged right now, odds are really good that you will be sometime in the future. That doesn't mean that you have to live your life in fear of what may or may not lie just around the corner. On the contrary, you have to always exist in the present. You have to take each event in life one step at a time—do the right thing, take a positive approach and possess the faith that everything is going to work out well in the end. Keep in mind that happiness is a choice you can make regardless of your circumstances. Choose to be happy, and then express that happiness with your actions.

I know it's going to work out for me. I'll guarantee it. That's the whole purpose of the challenge, to prepare me for the end. And when I do reach that point, I'll have a big smile on my face, because I will be absolutely positive of one thing...

More to come.

Resources

National Parkinson Foundation
200 SE 1st Street, Suite 800
Miami, FL 33131
www.parkinson.org
1-800-4PD-INFO (473-4636)

The Michael J. Fox Foundation for Parkinson's Research
Grand Central Station
P.O. Box 4777
New York, NY 10163-4777
www.michaeljfox.org
1-800-708-7644

Afterword

Speak Your Truth

"In the end, we will remember not the words of our enemies, but the silence of our friends." ~Rev. Martin Luther King, Jr.

I believe that every one of us is bestowed with an internal wisdom comprised of lifetimes of knowledge that shape our personal beliefs and individual view of the world. This wisdom acts as a compass, helping us navigate our way through life. It is the voice in our soul that speaks to our heart with intuitive words that influence our choices and initiate our actions. For each of us, it is the essence of who we are.

For many people, that essence is a light that burns brightly, fueled by love and compassion. The riches that are afforded them are not in what they receive but rather in what they give away—their service to others and their compassion for humanity. They have come to know the truth, that the spirit of the Divine does not exist in the ego of "I", but rather in the limitless sum of us all, for we all are truly of one universe, one source.

That same reality and potential for understanding and being exists in everyone. It's there; it just requires a reawakening of your own personal wisdom, your inner truth, and an understanding of who you are and why you are here. It requires letting go of ego and self. It also requires courage—a tremendous amount of courage.

Sharing your deepest, personal, intimate thoughts about life and what you feel and believe in your heart takes courage. There is most definitely fear associated with opening up to other people. We fear being vulnerable. We fear judgment and ridicule. Yet, what we fear sharing is our own truth. It's what each and every one of us believes, in our heart and in our soul, which guides us from day to day. It's a natural wisdom we are born with and carry with us for all eternity. It's a unique gift we all are capable of sharing if we can just overcome our fears.

For me to open up publicly and share my thoughts and feelings regarding Parkinson's and spirituality, as I have, was definitely frightening. I was very cognizant from the start, and I still am to this day, of not wanting to preach to anyone, but rather, to simply find a comfort in sharing the truth that exists in my heart, and speaking from a place of love and compassion— nothing more.

It's one thing to hear the voice that speaks to you, but it is entirely another to allow it to speak to others. Far too often, ego and fear stifle our voice of love and compassion.

As human beings, no better than the next, we often bear witness to racial injustices, as well as violence and bullying, turning a blind eye rather than lending a hand to those being suppressed. We avoid eye contact with the homeless as if to deny their existence; yet for them, feeling a sense of belonging to the social fabric is one of the most basic needs of humanity. If monetary assistance is beyond one's means, a genuine and heart-felt smile can often shine as brightly as a quarter.

We all must come to the realization that our spiritual beings are just renting space here in our earthly bodies. Once we can grasp that, we need to re-enter our world with a more open and giving heart.

If you feel love in your heart, speak of love. If you feel compassion, be compassionate. Live your life as it was intended, in harmony with mankind, not in silence due to fear and insecurity. Don't swallow the injustice you see in the world. It will only make you sick in the end. Taste the sweetness of your spirit and share it with everyone who hungers.

Let the first ripple of love start from you.

Speak your truth.

Made in the USA
Lexington, KY
02 August 2016